Mrs. Right

A woman's guide to becoming and remaining a wife

Tony A. Gaskins Jr.

Library of Congress Cataloging-in-Publication Data

Tony A. Gaskins Jr.,
Mrs. Right: A woman's guide to becoming and remaining a wife
Edited by: Karen R. Thomas
Published by: Soul Writers, LLC: PO Box 291835 Tampa, FL 33687

Library of Congress Control Number: 2012902336

ISBN: 978-0-9844822-4-5

10 9 8 7 6 5 4 3 2 1

Printed in the United States of America

Note: This book is intended only as an informative guide for those wishing to know about love. Readers are advised to consult a professional relationship coach or counselor before making any changes in their love life. The reader assumes all responsibility for the consequences of any actions taken based on the information presented in this book. The information in this book is based on the author's research and experience. Every attempt has been made to ensure that the information is accurate; however, the author cannot accept liability for any errors that may exist. The facts and theories on love and relationships are subject to interpretation, and the conclusions and recommendations presented here may not agree with other interpretations.

Contents

Introduction

It's my hope that this book will help women who are looking for answers in the relationship department. Every day I coach men and women on how to get it right and sometimes it feels like a never-ending journey. There are no quick and easy ways to find true love. I believe that God made love in the oven, not the mircrowave. It takes a lot of time and work to create the love that will last a lifetime. I've had more experience with women than I should have. I made a lot of mistakes and I broke a lot of hearts on my journey to finding true love. Along the way I took notes and I learned some very valuable lessons. I've come to the conclusion that women have a lot more power than men. If women understood this power it will help our relationships succeed much more often. We point the blame a lot but what it comes down to is each individual accepting responsibility for their actions. If you learn how to accept responsibility, then you will be surprised with the changes you see.

The information I share in this book is based on several years of personal studies and hundreds of hours of coaching men and women on relationships. I do not pull punches or sugar coat the truths that I've realized throughout my studies, so please brace yourself. So many women have asked me for the unadulterated truth but then refuse to take heed when they actually hear it. The women who have taken heed have succeeded. Not everything in the book will be for you so chew the meat and spit out the bones. This book wasn't written for one specific type of woman, but for several types of women. Some things will be common sense to you but to another woman it may be a divine revelation. Get what's for you and leave the rest. This book will not to be solution to all of your problems or will it answer every question you may have, so please don't depend solely on this book. Take initiative and sign up for coaching after you've read this book and continue the learning and growing process. Don't worry about what the men are doing or what they are learning. Take accountability for your life and worry about how you will carry yourself. Understand that if your head is on straight then it doesn't matter where a man is in his life because he can't do anything to you that you don't allow. This book will help you see men in a different light and understand yourself and the opposite sex much better. When the truth hurts the most that is where it needs to be embraced the most in order to see real results. So when you get to a point that you disagree with what's happening, really explore that feeling—most likely it's some type of insecurity or an area of your life that you need to address. It may be appearance, it may be attitude, or it may be your work habits. There are several topics covered in this book and something somewhere in this read is bound to strike you. So, pay attention and don't run from a truth that you may need to face head on!

Lastly, break the book down in sections. Although this is a quick read there is a lot of deep insight in this book that really needs to be pondered on to be fully understood, so take your time. Take notes and don't hesitate to contact me if you need to go deeper. This book isn't a quick ploy to make money and those who know much about the publishing industry know that on average being an author is not a way to get rich. Instead this book is my attempt to level the playing field and make women aware of how to better their relationship experience. This book is written from my heart, not just my head and the intention is to move our society forward and help create healthy and long lasting relationships.

May your journey be enriched by this read!

Oh, and remember, mistakes are human! So please excuse any mistakes you find in this book. We searched and searched but I'm convinced we maybe missed one or two. ☺

I

❧ *Fix You First!* ❧

"Insecurities in a relationship are like termites in a house…
slowly but surely they will destroy it."

1

🎕 *Healing Before Dealing* 🎕

"Only people without love say that love
isn't everything…love yourself."

O ne of the worst offenses a woman can commit is to carry the baggage from her last relationship into her new one—but it's almost impossible not to do. They always say, "Forgive but not forget;" well, to remember is to constantly relive what you have struggled through. If you don't forgive your past, then you won't have a future. I've heard the same proverb in many forms: "Forgiveness is a gift you give to yourself." Forgiveness is one of our most important and powerful tools for building a good relationship. We all need to move on from our failures without losing our enthusiasm for life. It's not easy, but it's not impossible either.

I like to examine common practices then dig and uncover why they exist. So I decided to do a quick study. I polled one hundred random women and asked them if they have ever taken the pain of the past into a new relationship. The results are below:

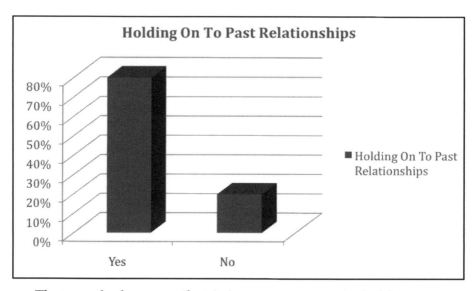

That graph shows us that it is very common to hold on to our past and drag that baggage with us into our future relationships. But most men do not like being a woman's problem solver. For a man, it's enough to have to solve the problems *he* is going to cause you. It's almost unfathomable to have to also solve the problems that another man caused. Not every man is the same and a woman has to be able to navigate past a hurt without carrying a burden. Otherwise, before you know it, your troubles will be too heavy, and no one will be able to hold you up. Women who carry the baggage from the past into the present are usually labeled needy, worrisome and are often victims of infidelity or just dumped altogether. Men fight internal battles every day just trying to be men and feel worthy of being called a Man. Having to decipher a woman's past problems and hurts sends a man into a place he never wants to visit, unless he is a paid therapist or life coach.

To begin the process of putting aside any past relationship baggage, it is paramount that you first forgive yourself.

Forgive yourself for falling for it. Forgive yourself for allowing yourself to be deceived. Forgive yourself for staying if you stayed through any of the drama. Forgive yourself for not being able to see it coming. All of those things really are not your fault, but women usually claim it as their own and carry the blame. Carrying blame is the heaviest thing you can bear, and usually no one wants to help you carry it. So forgive yourself for assuming that any of it was your fault. What a man does is completely out of your control. A man does not cheat or beat because you make him; he does those things because he is weak and something is utterly wrong with him. You cannot blame yourself for his mistakes and his wrongdoings. He will have his own karma for his actions. Whatever goes around comes around. Your own karma will be sweeter if what you send around is forgiveness to both yourself and him.

I remember going through what was really my karma, but it still felt like it would kill me. I am sure many women can relate to this type of pain because what happened to me is what usually happens to a woman.

I was attending college in a small town in West Virginia. I started dating a woman whom I met in the library. I was studying and she was studying, and I looked up and she was sucking a lollipop and smirking at me provocatively. Eventually, I approached her and we started talking. We decided to go back to her room and chill. We ended up having sex that same night. I had no intention of keeping in touch with what I thought was a one-night stand. Closing the deal so easily in the bedroom made it almost impossible for me to have any respect for her. Women may call it chemistry, but I call it anatomy. We did not have a connection; she was just insecure and looking for love in all the wrong places. I planned to move on, but the next night I wasn't doing anything, she sent me a message and we ended up hanging out again. She contacted me regularly, and I kept finding myself without plans, so I continued sleeping with her. Eventually, I started meeting other people and wondered what it would be like to be with them. So naturally, I started sleeping with other women. This woman did everything to stay relevant in my life, so we started "dating." I had no other real potential mates, so I settled for what I could get at the time. Considering that she lost my respect on the first night we met, I participated in this relationship to use her car, spend her money, and have sex whenever I wanted it. I realize that I am being very frank about it, but wouldn't life be so much easier if men did not lie and lead you on? As time passed, I started cheating on her with whatever females I met who interested me. I always tried to sleep with them on the first night to see if they would respect themselves and say no, or give in to my coercion. I'd say 95% of them gave in on the first night. I was shocked by my ability to easily close the deal with little to no effort.

Eventually, my girlfriend and I started getting really serious and I suppose I developed true feelings for her. I think I started caring for her because she remained by my side through all of the games and lies. She did anything I asked of her and she rarely questioned me. I should have had suspicions, but I didn't. After we were "engaged" my college football teammates began hinting to me that she was being unfaithful just as I had been to her. I could not fathom this. I had conditioned my mind to believe that under no circumstance would she cheat on me like I had cheated on her. I had convinced myself that I was God's gift to women and there was no way that this really plain-Jane female would cheat on a handsome, well-built specimen like me. It may sound conceited but this was seriously what I had tricked myself to believe. It turned out that I was very wrong. Not only had she cheated on me, but also she had cheated with my teammates. I believe it was four teammates, five guys in total. My stomach turns just writing this even though it happened eight years ago. I was devastated! I cried like a little baby. I couldn't sleep, I couldn't eat, I couldn't think. I was torn to pieces. The karma train had arrived to my station! Everything I had sown since I was fifteen had now become what I was reaping. I finally was able to feel what it feels like when I would cheat on her. I once heard that the taste of a man's own medicine might kill him. I know now what that really means.

Destiny separated us because she flunked out of school. She was too focused on other things so she was unable to maintain acceptable grades. I took that opportunity to exit the relationship. I knew from day one that it never should have been; the relationship had been like an experiment for both of us. Nevertheless, it left me emotionally scarred—the way a lot of women have been scarred, but I honestly believe that women are much stronger than men, so my healing process took much longer. I did not forgive her, I did not forgive myself, and I dragged that hurt and anger into my next two relationships. The next relationship I ruined because I was not able to trust her. I invaded her privacy; I dictated her life and transformed into an abusive boyfriend. It was all because I could not trust myself, so I projected those suspicions onto everyone else. The next relationship ended after two years and then I met my wife. Initially, I even ruined that relationship. I couldn't trust her either. But the woman who would become my wife was much too strong to stick around and let a man control her life and invade her privacy, so she left. Months later, we rekindled our relationship, but that journey required time, effort and trust.

It wasn't until I forgave myself, forgave my ex and made a vow that I would love brand new that I was able to stop hurting and pushing away others. My father, a pastor and an awesome life coach, told me, "Son, you have to love like you've never been hurt before and be willing to be hurt again." At the time, that didn't make much sense to me, but I decided to try it and I must admit, loving like that felt so good. I told myself that I would trust my woman until she caused me to lose trust in her.

We are all human and we all make mistakes. It would feel much better if we could go to our partners in confidence and admit our wrongs; knowing that we will be forgiven and given the chance to start over fresh and make it right. I am not speaking of cheating alone; I am also speaking of small, seemingly harmless things like little lies about finances. These are the types of things that partners hide because their mates are too torn and hurt from the past that every chance that presents itself, they hurt the ones who love them. Forgive your past and start brand new. It is such a liberating feeling.

Time heals all wounds

I asked one hundred people how much time they allow themselves between relationships, 0-6 months, 6 months to a year, or 1 year or more. Fifty percent said 0-6 months. Thirty percent said 6 months to a year, and only twenty percent said they wait one year or more.

That was a very small glimpse into how most people go from relationship to relationship without taking adequate time to heal. When you move from person to person looking for someone to complete you, they usually end up *de*pleting you instead. Imagine a broken object flying through the air and it keeps hitting other objects. Picture that each time it hits another object, a piece of it breaks off. Eventually, that object will be completely destroyed with pieces scattered everywhere. This is how some individuals end up, broken and scattered. Before I built a solid relationship, this was the way I operated myself, and as a professional relationship coach, I have coached many people who've operated this way.

So often we get accustomed to being with someone and depending on someone else to meet our emotional needs. We end up forgetting how to be alone. We forget how to be a whole person all by ourselves. We feel like we are only half a person and that we need someone else to make us whole. That is a lie we tell ourselves and unfortunately, that lie has ruined so many people. We get in a relationship, we get hurt and then we run to someone else to cover up the pain or fill that void in our lives, not realizing that running to the wrong person will just make it worse. This is especially true for women because many men are seeking women whom they can take advantage of and dominate. When a weak and insecure man is looking for a mate, he is looking for a woman who has lost her self-esteem and self-worth. He lacks these characteristics also, but he knows that because he is the physically stronger vessel, he can overpower the woman with coercion by fear or manipulation by guilt. He uses his craftiness to suck her in and then suck her dry, leaving her dependent on him. The French author Francois De La

Rochefoucauld wrote, "Oftentimes we are more treacherous through weakness than through calculation." Acting in weakness, people hurt other people. Caught up in that kind of cycle, we see so many women who are addicted to drama and pain. These same women then start saying that love is pain and that love hurts. In actuality, true love is the opposite of pain and hurt. But if we do not take the time to heal and love ourselves and really get to know love by first loving ourselves, then someone will come along and teach us how to hate ourselves and we will confuse the two.

Unfortunately, right after a bad breakup, many women turn to another man to soothe the pain of what the last man did to them. These women do not realize that pain is a healing agent. Let me explain what I mean by that. When we injure ourselves physically, it's the pain that calls our attention to that injury and lets us know something needs our care—and we need to be conscious of that injury until it has had time to heal. If we didn't feel pain we might not give our injury due attention and necessary care, and could worsen the injury or even cause ourselves permanent damage. Our emotional wounds are no different. The pain—our grief, our aching heart—tells us to allow ourselves the time to heal our heart and mind. If we don't take that time, the wound will stay open and it will just get worse. When you accept pain as part of the healing process, you come out on the other end tougher than you were before. Sometimes we have to "*go* through to *get* to." Pain is a healing agent; don't run from it, come *through* it. Give yourself time to think, to meditate, to cry, to hurt, and most importantly, to heal.

It's a cliché that tells us time heals all things, and I believe that if you look back over your life, you will know that it's true. Whenever you were hurt, if you gave yourself time and space to heal and you allowed time to treat that wound, most likely, you didn't hurt as bad on Day Seventy as you did on Day Seven.

Start fresh and change your approach:

It's not possible to go back and relive the past, but we can start brand new in the present. We can go past any failure without losing enthusiasm. It's not about never being hurt; we will all be hurt at some point in our lives. It's about being able to get over the circumstance or the person who has hurt us. By starting fresh I do not mean to keep starting fresh in the same toxic relationship. Don't be confused. I would never tell anyone to stay with someone who continuously hurts them. Starting fresh means that after you have ended a bad relationship and taken the time to heal, you will move forward without carrying any anger, bitterness, hurt or mistrust. You will begin as if you've never been hurt. Take on the next relationship brand new, a little more mature, a little wiser, and a little more prepared. Be optimistic, be hopeful, but change your approach and also be smart and be careful. Starting fresh isn't meant to imply that you should be blind to the signs.

Many times women go from bad relationship to bad relationship because they failed to do something different from one ex to the next. Don't just go through life; *grow* through life. Learn from the mistakes of your last relationship and be determined not to repeat them. If you've seen a person go through two or three abusive relationships back to back it's because they did not learn and apply. Knowledge is only power if you apply it. If in your last relationship you failed to heed the warning signs that your man was a cheater or beater, make sure in the next that you are fully aware of those red flags. That way if you see them, you are able to pull back right away instead of getting to the point of no return and feeling like you are obligated or stuck in a relationship that is going south.

You can heal from the pain of the past. Time heals all wounds. Be patient. Be kind to yourself and start loving yourself all over again. Take your time and learn what real love is. If you rush it, you will ruin it. There is a great man in preparation for you right now. You can't force love, you must first become love and then you will attract love. Just like after every storm there's a rainbow, after every hurt there is healing. Take your time moving forward and let the necessary occur.

2

❦ *Are You Relationship Ready?* ❦

From a very young age, many women dream of being in a relationship, but the sad part is that a fairy tale is much different from reality. Men don't have that same type of dream growing up, so when the time comes our reality is much different than that woman's dream. Most women only see the Cinderella wedding in their head and they fail to think of all the behind the scenes duties and chores that a man will ask of them once the honeymoon is over. In this day and time women are becoming very successful and very ambitious. The things that used to be the norm are no more. Women are becoming more successful than many men. More than ever before women are attending college and getting degrees and then climbing the corporate ladder. Women are getting used to being single and embracing that role as an independent woman but still dreaming of meeting prince charming. The question is: are you ready for what prince charming has in mind for you?

The Cheerleader: Contrary to popular belief most men do not have an ego that requires a woman to knock them from their high horse. In fact most men are very insecure in their ability as a man and need encouragement and a lot of support. From the day he was born he had a mother that was there for him and looked out for his every need. If it wasn't his mother then most likely it was another female figure. She supported him in his endeavors and cheered him on along the way. He became dependent on the reassurance that he was on the right track and this support system became vital to his success in life. When a man gets ready to settle down with that special lady he wants to know that she will cheer him on. He wants to know that she will have his back through thick and thin and be there as his backbone to support him and help him stay up. Picture the role of the cheerleader at a game that's how a lot of men view it in a relationship. While he is playing in the game of life he wants to know that his lady will cheer him on and be in his ear when he's falling behind or his morale is low. I can see the face of many women reading this. One type of woman has her mouth curled up and her brows furrowed and eyes squinted and saying to herself, *what do I look like? Can I not have a life of my own?* The answer is YES! The other type of woman is smiling and saying to herself, *I got this. I can do this with no problem. I love to support my man.* Which woman are you? The latter will be the choice of your average man. The first will be the choice of the man who is very mature, understanding, and easy going. These two men will carry themselves differently and they will produce different results for their household. It's important that you decide which woman are you and what type of man you want to attract. The man who is okay with his lady being as busy as or busier than him isn't very common but there are some that exist. This picture I just painted is one that I see all the time. As a relationship coach, I hear the complaints from women and men about this very topic everyday. I believe that every woman will come to that point in her life where she won't mind being a cheerleader for her man and being able to support him everyday in the game of life. If that time isn't now then I suggest you not try to rush into a relationship or be desperate for love because just a fast as you find it you can lose it.

The Soccer Mom: One thing men dream about is seeing what their seed will look like. Men get bored very easily. As soon as he gets used to a woman and he doesn't feel that there is much more he wants to figure out then he decides he wants to have kids. The beauty about this is that most women want children also. This scenario usually works out perfectly while the couple is trying to conceive the child. Then when the child is actually born, things begin to get a little rocky. Men do not fully understand the changes a woman's body goes through during pregnancy and childbirth. We are just simply along for the ride and watching in amazement at how a woman's body changes and grows. We see a woman go from the woman we once adored to the woman that we thought we'd never be with. I'm speaking for the majority of men as I know it so please don't be offended. To most men pregnancy isn't beautiful, cute, or adorable. It's rather strange and mind boggling, but we cope with it the best we can. I'm sure as a woman you've heard horror stories from other women about how their man started cheating on them during those nine months. I hear them all the time and it's quite sad. The reason is because men are visual creatures and most men do not appreciate the wonders of childbirth so therefore they are no longer attracted to the woman that is in front of them and that can cause for wandering eyes. Sheesh, this is getting a bit harsh. I really wish I could paint a fairytale but because I deal with these things daily I can only report the truth. Men want the production but don't understand or appreciate the process. We want the icing off of the cake but don't appreciate the time and sweat it took to make this masterpiece. So therefore men simply insert their tool, let it do what it's supposed to do and then cross their fingers and try to get by for nine months and pick up the beautiful gift that you've just made. Then even worse than that is that after you've had the baby and it's time to come home things get even crazier. Your body is tired and needs to rest but you have this screaming hungry baby who needs to be fed every couple of hours and a man who is walking around looking like he's from another planet. Your body is begging you for some rest and relaxation but this baby is asking for the same thing and it's highly unlikely that both of you will get it at the same time. This is where a good man comes in handy but most men become a space cadet at this time and every time you need him he's always zoned out. Now you find yourself having to get up in the middle of the night to feed the baby, change diapers, and soothe the crying and he only shows up to play with the baby and then put the baby back in your arms when the crying starts again. On top of that, he wants you to do this two or three more times. Okay, that was a very vivid picture and it was very honest. If you don't believe it then ask a woman who has a child and is still with her man. You will find a few women who say their man helped out a whole lot, but most will say, *girl all he did was play with the baby when it was convenient for him and then leave me to clean up the mess but I still love him.* Now that's the real deal for you! Ironically, that man who does that is a pretty decent man. He may be faithful, hard working, and compassionate, but men just aren't built with the sensitivity towards emotions like women are and that's a scientific fact. There are always exceptions to the rule, but I must prepare you by the rules not the exceptions. The beauty about this is that YOU CAN DO IT!! Many women have had this very thing happen to them and they made it, not to mention the many women who did it completely on their own. So please don't let this ruin your idea of this perfect relationship.

CEO of Home, LLC: The average man, the ones you will run into most often will still be stuck in gender roles. He will believe that it's his job to go out and hunt for the food, bring it back to a clean house and then have you prepare it and then clean up after it's over. He will feel that it's his job to work and pay bills and take care of the lawn, and the trash and maintenance around the house but your job to cook, clean, and take care of the kids. The problem with that is that many women today have spent years in college racking up school loans and have dreams of climbing the corporate ladder. Guess what? You have every right to do just that! But where does he fit in? There are some men, who can get past that, but usually those men are the ones who have went through my six-week course on love *called For The Love of Me,* or something like it and learned what being a real man is. The average man hasn't done so and he will expect what he expects! Is it wrong? As a woman, that's up to you to decide, after you understand what type of woman are you. Some women don't mind balancing it all. Some women would rather make a lot of money and hire a nanny, and the rest don't really care and just say they will figure it out when the time comes. It will do you much more good to know going in what type of woman you are so you know what type of man you will allow into your life. I have to hear from a woman everyday that she is upset because she wants to pursue her dreams but her husband wants her to be bionic woman and work forty hours a week, keep a spotless house, cook dinner every night, and have the kids in tip top shape while he just comes home and sits down until dinner is ready. Then he leaves a mess, goes into the bathroom to shower and leaves his underwear for her to pick up and after all of that he wants to have sex. Whoa!!!!!! That's a lot to ask for, isn't it? But guess what? That's a normal guy. He's not a pig, or a punk, or a loser, he's a normal everyday average guy whom America has told this is the way it's supposed to be. Can you handle that? Or will you try to work something out or talk some sense into him? The beauty about it is that YOU CAN DO IT, if you want to. As a woman you don't really know all that you are capable doing until you are put to the test and I guarantee you will even surprise yourself. Is this fair? NO, not at all!! Is it real? Yes, it is very much so!

I know for most women this section just rubbed you the wrong way and you are contemplating if you want to continue reading this misogynistic, chauvinistic, and all the other "istic's" you can think of, type-of-book but I assure you that I don't think that this should be the role of the woman. I'm just simply trying to prepare you for what could become your reality, even with a "good" man. On the other end, I will be telling men not to be this way in my book for men. Just in case it doesn't get through, I want you to know what could be in store for you so that you are fully aware and prepared. I want you to know that there is nothing wrong with having dreams and wanting to make money and be your own boss. I commend you for those things. However, you must realize that most men want a family, a very secure and sound home structure and if you are doing what he is doing (working hard to make money and reach personal milestones in the workplace) then it may not sit well with him. Most men are looking for a woman who is the missing piece to his puzzle, but if you are working just as hard as him, he will see you as "friend material," but not "wifey material." It's my hope that if you don't want to become the type of woman you just read about, you can find a man who doesn't want you to be that woman either. However, I will be honest with you and let you know that they aren't swarming in the streets. They will be few and far in between mainly because of how society has molded their ideas of family structure.

Do not be discouraged in the slightest bit. Instead be encouraged and know that there is a time for everything and this may be your time to grind and there will come a day when you don't want to work as hard and family life will be more appealing to you. At the same time there are some stories that prove that you can have your cake and eat it to and if you are fortunate you just may be that lucky woman to get that. My wife is able to pursue her passions and be a mom and the CEO of our household so I know it's possible and it happens every day. The house isn't always as clean as I'd like it to be and dinner isn't always made, but I realize that if I want something done I can pitch in and help. And if I won't help then I know to shut my mouth and not complain about it. I accept that my wife is human and what she can and can't do. I also accept the same about myself. So I know that if it can be done in my household it can be done in other households also.

3

❧ As You Dress ❧
You'll Be Addressed

C lothes send statements that oftentimes the sender isn't aware of. How is the person receiving it? Perception is key not only in relationships but also in life. Usually a man judges a woman based on how she presents herself. Men are simple creatures yes, but not when it comes to judging a woman. From your hair to your shoes, every item you have on sends a message to a man. He receives it and then decodes it in his own way and then passes a judgment on your character, your career, and the possibilities of you being a potential mate. This may sound unfair, but we all do it to some extent, men and women. I conducted a recent study of 100 men of different races and nationalities and asked them would they respect a woman who had on a very revealing outfit and see her as a potential wife, eighty percent of the men said NO.

Then I asked the men would they be attracted to a woman in a very revealing outfit enough to date and sleep with her with no intentions of marrying her, seventy percent of the men said yes.

Lastly I asked the men would they prefer their wife to dress sexy and revealing or sexy but conservative, ninety-two percent of the men said sexy and conservative.

Before I conducted, this study I had an idea of how the men would answer because I'm a man. But I wanted to make sure that this wasn't just my opinion and that the majority of men had similar beliefs. I found out that I wasn't too far off. You see society has determined what is classy and what is not—men usually accept those ideas as their own beliefs. I want to break down some of the messages that appearance sends to a man.

Hair

➤ Long flowing hair: Long flowing hair tells a man that this woman is sophisticated and likes the finer things in life. Any man who has dated before knows that it cost money to flat iron, straighten, wash, relax, condition, trim, add extensions or highlights to hair. Men who have paid for a woman to get her hair done like this could have spent $100-$250 depending on the length and if she had anything added like color or extensions. This is a clear message to most men and a man who doesn't want a "high maintenance" woman may look pass this woman as a potential mate. That is if he intends to be the one paying for the hair appointments. This hairstyle also says to a man that this woman could be conceited or likes attention because of the attention long flowing hair usually attracts. Wise men know that this isn't always true, but if he doesn't have the time to find out he may over look her and keep walking. A wealthy man or a man who can afford the hair appointments may be interested in this type of woman. This type of man doesn't see the expense as a problem and this look would be great arm candy. Long flowing hair won't deter all "broke" men, just the ones who are looking for a serious mate and want to be the sole provider. Yes ladies, it gets that deep even though some men may not be able to articulate this.

➤ The short "bob" cut: This cut is typically worn by quiet or reserved women, therefore many men may see this haircut as inviting because the woman may seem like a "weaker vessel" or docile individual. They believe this woman can be led or molded into the type of woman he wants. Of course there are exceptions, but based on the studies we held this is what most men felt.

➤ The "Halle Berry Cut": This haircut is the really low cut where the sides and back are pressed to the scalp and low. When a man see's this type of woman he is most likely to believe she is the strong, feisty type. This type of woman is usually daring and willing to take chances, henceforth she cut off all of her hair and wears it with pride instead of putting on a wig.

➤ The Bun: This hairstyle says to a man that a woman is conservative and likes to keep it mostly natural. The bun isn't a real attention grabber, but it can be done with style. It implies that the woman is confident, but not conceited.

➤ The long curls: This hairstyle when worn by a white female suggest to black males that she would date outside of her race because she is going against the norm with her hair style. My personal experiences suggest this also. For a black female to have curls in her hair says that she is classy, stylish and elegant. If this hairstyle is with extensions then it could go hand in hand with the long flowing hair. If it's natural curls from wetting the hair then it suggest something totally different. That suggests that the woman is natural and comfortable in her own skin and embraces her natural beauty.

Some may be surprised that a woman's hair could send so many messages, but it can. Even from the days of old our hairstyles have said a lot about whom a person was and how they felt about themselves.

Tops:

➢ Low cut shirt: this tells a man that a woman is comfortable with her physique and knows where her assets lie and doesn't mind showing them off. It could also mean that's she's insecure with who she is on the inside so she needs to catch a man with her body. It's a toss up but this is what goes through the mind of most men.

➢ High-collared shirt: this tells a man that this woman could have a nice upper body but even if she does she isn't trying to show it off to get attention. She would rather hide what she doesn't have, or leave what she does have to the imagination. It could also suggest that she is very conservative, taken, or not looking to impress men.

➢ Belly shirt: This shirt doesn't allow a man to really take a woman seriously because it suggests that she is all a show and she wants attention from every man that she walks past.

Shoes:

> ➤ Flats: this is typical of a conservative woman that likes to be comfortable and classy. This suggests to a man that a woman either doesn't have much style, or she is already taken and doesn't want much attention. Flats could also make a woman seem like a plain-Jane, but that isn't a bad thing for a man that wants a woman to marry him. Many men don't want a woman that seems like she is addicted to attention; instead they seek one that is subtle with her beauty.

> ➤ Sneakers: these shoes tell a man that the woman could have an athletic side to her and that she also likes to be comfortable. Women who wear sneakers out and about are the type of woman that a man feels comfortable with, and doesn't feel like he has a certain standard to live up to. He can just be himself.

> ➤ 3-inch heels: the shoes suggest that a woman has a sense of style but isn't trying to overdo it. She isn't necessarily looking for attention; she just likes to look classy and elegant without being too forward with her attempt.

> ➤ 4-6 inch heels: these shoes tell a man that this woman doesn't mind being looked at. She also has a strong sense of style and likes to be fashionable. This could also suggest to a man that she is high maintenance or could be a hard act to keep up with. All types of women wear heels, and most men understand that and are very attracted to a woman in high heels. A strong secure man who is ambitious and likes the finer things in life doesn't mind a woman who wears heels. A man who is

height challenged and could have a complex would most likely lust after, but not approach a woman in high heels.

A woman's clothes suggest a lot to a man. It says a lot about how she views herself and what she is looking for in the world. Our society has largely shaped how we view women when it comes to how she dresses and men analyze this before they say a word to a woman.

Picture a stripper and her outfit. Strippers are what men turn to for a fun night out. Men idolize the bodies of strippers and pay good money to see and some even pay for sexual favors from the strippers. Strippers are usually women who need more money than they think they have the means of making another way so in a sense they "use what they have, to get what they want." Men realize that and take advantage of that need. Strippers start out in a very short dress or miniskirt, similar to what some women wear out to a night club, and then they take off one piece at a time. Men subconsciously keep that idea in their mind when viewing women in public. The closer a woman is dressed to a stripper then the less respect a man has for her. He feels like she is degrading herself, and she wants attention at any cost. Therefore he touches her inappropriately, speaks to her inappropriately or feels like he can buy her since she appears to be "selling" her body by showing so much of it. Sometimes women forget that when they go out to a nightclub and have a lot of skin showing. Many are thinking it's a cute dress and it'll get them some attention and that'll be it. Little do they know, men are viewing them from a totally different perspective with the picture of a stripper in the back of his mind.

Then women get the unwelcomed grab of the butt cheek, or the whistle or funny sounding call that sounds like the man is calling some type of animal. Most women have a look on their face like they are very offended that they can't come to the club with the bottom of their butt cheeks showing and drink in peace. I've seen several men get slapped in a nightclub for misreading a woman's outfit. Is it his fault? Many would say no. Then some would say that still doesn't give him the right to touch her or disrespect her just because she has butt cheeks showing or a nipple playing "peek-a-boo." This is all very confusing to a lot of men because they are under the impression that this woman wants this kind of attention, while the woman could just be under the impression that this is a very sexy dress that makes her feel good about her body. This is why it's so important to understand perception.

So because strippers seem to have sold their self-worth and they don't wear many clothes, men associate women who wear revealing clothes in public with strippers. I've seen many women who wear the same type of clothes a stripper wears in public but they would never consider stripping. They are just trying to look sexy. Then there are strippers who may dress sexy and conservative when not at work and men are surprised to find out what they really do for a living. It all boils down to what type of messages are you sending and how are they being received. So when you ask yourself why can't I dress revealing and be respected like everyone else, that is the answer. Dress how you want to be addressed.

Then on the other hand, we have corporate jobs where women wear business suits or slacks and nice blouses. So, because of those outfits men associate class and self-worth with a woman who dresses like a corporate businesswoman. There is a fine line between being classy and being boring in the mind of a man, but most men won't look that deep into it. Business casual always suggest that a woman has a respectable job or is in pursuit of one and she knows who she is and she respects herself. So when it's time to get serious in a man's life this is what he is looking for in a woman. Then when he is looking to just have fun or have sex, he's looking for the type of woman who is dressed closer to a stripper. This should begin to make some sense to you.

Women often ask; why do men fall for the stripper or Barbie type? That's because they look like a good time. They look fun and daring with little inhibition and not much ambition to be blunt. They look like they are trying to win the attention of a man and that they want to be "bought" or scooped up for a good time and more often than not that's exactly how men treat them. If you think about it, you'll notice that most of the notable stripper and Barbie type may have had a handsome boyfriend but it only lasted two years or less. That's because the men went in with no real intentions of settling down and getting married as the graph showed you earlier. They just wanted to come in, make it look convincing to her, have a good time and leave. It's a cold world, I know but that is how the game is often played so dress warm.

Who ultimately wins? The majority of the time, the winner will be the woman who dresses like she loves and respects herself and knows what she wants out of life. The woman who dresses closer to the corporate America woman is the one who usually ends up with the ring. It doesn't mean she works in corporate America and is a strong and powerful businesswoman, it simply means she carries herself like she could be. The women who dress more like a stripper does, well they have a good time but end up losing out. Those are the women that get a lot of the flights around the world, the cool vacations, the expensive gifts, but then are left lonely and heart broken because they thought that this way was going to work. We often see men cheat on their corporate America dressing girlfriend or wife with the "fun time" stripper-dressing lady on the side. It can be a win-lose sometimes, but when you stick to your values and meet the right man it'll become a win-win. Remember values may change, but principles remain the same. Although some "dogs" stray away for the day they'll find their way back home. I'm not suggesting that you allow a man to cheat; I'm simply saying that if you wait it out for a good man and you respect yourself while waiting, you win!

II
Your Past Affects Your Present

"Just like with our jobs, we have a resume for our relationships and a man will want to see it."

4

🎋 *How Your Past Affects* 🎋 *Your Present with a Man*

Numerous sex partners: I talk to men all the time in relationship coaching sessions where there main concern is a woman's past. Men have this King-like mentality that makes us want a "Queen." A woman who is as pure as possible, but yet we may be filthy dirty. It's another societal condition that men have bought into. A man may have had 50+ sexual partners in his lifetime and a woman accepts that and considers it normal. I know men who have had 300+ sexual partners and are married now to a woman who doesn't consider their past at all. Now in this day and time we are hearing more and more men become forgiving of the past, at least all the way up until it's time to get married. There always comes that conversation where the man wants to talk about how many past relationships and sexual partners you've had. Why? Why should he worry about or even care about who you've been with? Well, it's called your **relationship resume.** A relationship resume is the list of all of your exes and all of your sexual partners. In that man's mind he is like the CEO of his company and he is interviewing you to see how you will fit into his company. Just like with a job, he wants to check your resume to determine whether you will be an asset or a liability. It is smart and it's also fair for a woman to do the same thing. My father always told me, *don't get mad if you hit someone and they hit you back harder.* The meaning of that really is that we can't expect someone to carry him or herself or accept things just because we would accept them. The man has a right to judge you before he brings you in his life, just as you have the right to equally judge him before you bring him in your life. If he's slept with three hundred women and you know his name is all around town for it and you ignore it and then he cheats on you; whose fault is that? Is it his fault for cheating or your fault for ignoring the warning signs? He showed you who he was and you should've believed him. Men are not as forgiving as women. Men have hard bottom lines but women can be a bit more flexible and understanding. With men it either is or it isn't. There is no middle ground. Again, I'm speaking of the rule not the exception. So to a man if you've had 10+ partners and they weren't all with men that you were in a committed relationship with then you are beginning to look different to that man. He is borderline seeing you as a little gullible or naïve. If you have 20+ partners now you are showing him signs of brokenness or confusion and a lack of self-worth. If you have 30+ partners he will believe that your line of work was sex and that you were pretty much getting paid to have sex or giving sex to "come up." Mind you, in this day there are many women who have 30+ sexual partners because we live in a very sexually charged society and it's seen as okay. The bad part is that those women are not taking into account how that will affect their future with their husband. To put it plainly, **men have issues with this!** Men will have nightmares about your past sexual partners. He will be having sex with you and picturing you with another man. You will be driving down the road with him and out of nowhere he will ask you was the sex better with such and such. You are totally thrown off and blown away by this insecurity, but yet it's almost normal for a man. Again, men struggle with their identity and living up to what the world expects them to be. So men often want to know how they measure up to your past boyfriends. Who was bigger? Who lasted the longest? Who made you feel the best? Things that you may never even think of asking your man—he wants to know! He wants to know who, when, and where, and why it happened, and if he's really insecure he may want to know what time of day it was. Some of you know exactly what I'm talking about, but if you are new to dating or haven't had much experience yet then your mouth is probably on the floor. Yes, this actually happens and I have to deal with it every day as a Relationship Coach. As a man, I was once that insecure man so I understand these men when they come to me talking about this and also the women who come to me blown away that he actually cares about all of these details. I did a poll of 100 men and asked them if they would marry a woman who had over ten sexual partners. Guess what? 90% said NO. As a man I wasn't really surprised because I know how men think, but the women who saw the poll were ap-palled and very upset at the double standard. I tell you, double standards don't exist unless you allow them to. Don't accept the double standard. If you don't want a man who has had more than ten sexual partners for reasons of safety and sanity then by all means do not accept a man like that. But if you do accept him do not by any means expect him to be as forgiving if you tell him the same thing. There are some men who will, but most men won't. Most men won't be forgiving because he knows the type of demons he will have to fight in his mind. Women can walk around with a man and even if she passes another woman that he has been with, you feel like, *oh well he's mine now.* Men on the other hand feel like crap if they walk by another man that you've been with. He feels embarrassed and less than a man. Even if he isn't being laughed at, he feels like he's being laughed at. If I had a dollar for every time I've heard that I'd be filthy rich.

Think about a Queen, she is raised to be a Queen all her life. She is chaste and pure and set aside to be a King's bride. That is what a man dreams about when he dreams about a wife. But the problem is that in our society we are not raising our daughters like that. We aren't instilling in them that "Queen-like" mentality. Also not many fathers are in the home and so therefore young women don't know their worth. Women are feeling like if they don't have sex, they'll be left behind and that's not true. It's actually the other way around. It's the women that have had too much sex that end up being left single and lonely in the end. She may have some long relationships and she may even get married and it last for a few years, but when a man thinks about that woman he's going to take on that last stretch of his life he wants her to be as pure as possible. That could mean ten or less men, or it could mean fifteen or less men in our time. Whatever it means he will seek to find the one who has tried to save herself as much as possible for the one she will die with.

Do not worry about the irony of it all. Don't get caught up in the double standard. Instead allow this section to help you understand that your present decisions will affect your future. Think about it very hard before you sleep with another man and raise your number. Know that there is a man that is waiting for you and he wants you to be all his and how many other men you've been with will weigh heavily on his decision. Is it fair? NO! Is it a reality? YES! I can't paint you a pretty picture and tell you that it'll be that way. I can't tell you that any man will accept you with 30+ sexual partners in your past because I would be telling you a lie. I am a man and I coach too many men to know that it's not true and I can't tell lies. I'm here to help not hurt. So my advice to you is to save yourself from here on out. Do not give yourself to a man sexually unless he's put in enough time and effort to make you think he will be your husband for life. I want you to know a secret about men. WE WILL WAIT ON YOU! A man who loves a woman will wait as long as it takes to have sex with her. If you say you aren't having sex until the honeymoon then that man will marry you first. If he leaves it's only because he never intended to stay in the first place. He just wanted to sell you a dream, have sex with you and find a reason to break up with you all along. Please stop falling for the okie-doke and raising your number. Having a sexual partner on your **relationship resume** is just like having job terminations on your job resume. Think of it like that and it will save you a lot of heartache. You are worth more than just sex! You are worth more than just a good time. You are worth more than lies and deceit. You are worth a RING. You are worth a lifetime commitment! You are worth a man's heart! You are worth a man that has saved himself just as much as you have saved yourself. You are worth all that and more! Do not accept less. It doesn't matter what you've been through at this point because no matter what it is, there is a man who will love you for you. But what you can do is begin now to create a better future by making better decisions in the present. You may be at thirty sexual partners right now, but you don't have to go to fifty. You can stop right here and start loving and respecting yourself and saving yourself for that ring and faithful marriage that you've always dreamed of having.

Baby Daddies: Men understand other men so they take it seriously when another man is still attached to you. Men will fight and some even kill over the woman they love. All men understand that about other men, so therefore baby daddies are not taken lightly. It takes a very special type of man to accept a woman and love her and her kid(s) if her child's father is still involved. If you have kids then it's already done and there is nothing you can do about it. I can tell you that it makes it just a little bit tougher to find a man, but it's not impossible. I know a lot of men that are with a woman who has kids and a few of them are good men and doing it for the right reasons. Most of those men have kids themselves. Therefore it's important that wherever you are in life as far as kids are concerned that you make sure the next one counts. You can't change the past but you can predict the future by what you do now. The key is to make a man commit. Otherwise you are just taking on extra responsibility and stacking the odds against you finding another man that will love you and another man's kids. That is the biggest issue I find with men being with a woman who already has children. Those men don't want to look another man's child in the eye everyday and have to pick up the slack that he left behind. A man would rather do that for his own child instead. So it presents a small problem. I can't count how many coaching calls I've been on with a man and he says, *but she has a kid.* It's tough for a woman to hear that, but that's your **traditional man.** The **new age man** is more understanding and he will accept a woman's kids and love them as his own. The **new age man** is usually one that longs for a family and he doesn't mind that a woman has kids as long as her head is on straight and that she has her child's father in place! He just wants a family, but be prepared to have kids with him also because as I said earlier most men want to see their own seed come to life. The **traditional man** on the other hand wants no parts of a woman with a child. He wants to start from scratch and build his own family. He doesn't believe in taking care of another man's kids and he doesn't want to see another man popping up at his house for visitation rights and having to interact with his wife. I will tell you from my studies that there are more traditional men than there are new age men.

The beauty about this situation is that if you have a child there are many men who have a child also. Sometimes it takes us a time or two to get it right and that's understandable, so now more than ever we are seeing more blended families. These families are working together well, especially if the kids are over the age of five, then it's even easier. So as a woman with a child you should put on your list that you want a man with a child. That way you don't have to deal with the stress and headaches that a **traditional man** will bring you. You want a man that is understanding of your situation and knows that not all relationships work out and that's why you have a child and you are not in a relationship with the father. With the right amount of relationship coaching the two of you can blend together just fine and actually bring strength to one another. The key is that wherever you are in life that you don't dig yourself into a deep hole. The more kids you have from different men without a real commitment then the more you stack the odds against yourself in trying to find a good man that will love you and your kids. Make a man give you a real commitment before having his child, and if he isn't willing to do that then he doesn't deserve to put a child in you! There are no guarantees, not even in marriage but at least know in your heart and soul that this man is for real. If you don't feel deep down that he is then don't go any further with him.

If you don't have any kids, then don't rush into it. Never think that having a man's child will make him step up and marry you or love you anymore than he already does. A child will not keep a man! A child will not make a man marry you. That is all up to that man. The best way to go about it is to save yourself, get a commitment in the form of something that is legally binding like a marriage, and then have his child. If you don't believe in marriage then baby, you are on your own. You are letting a man enter you with absolutely no reason to stay with you. It's the most risky way to conceive a child and that is the very reason why we have so many single moms. We have been conditioned to have sex first and then talk about marriage later and because we are doing it backwards our society and our kids are suffering the consequences. We have to bring back the sound societal structure and remember that the principles have not changed, only our values. Don't let your values change with society; instead let your values change society.

Ex-husbands: Although it seems very similar to a baby daddy an ex-husband is very different in a man's eye. The reason being is because an ex-husband means that you had a legally binding, holy union with a man that was calculated and thought out. That means it was serious and the fact that you all have severed ties means that you are through for good. This sends a totally different message to a man than having a baby daddy. With a baby daddy a man will think that there is a possibility he will keep running in and out of your life. An ex-husband on the other hand means that you all have given it your best shot and it didn't work out. It also solidifies in that man's mind that you are wife material because a man has already chosen you to be his bride, and if the divorce was the man's fault then the new guy would respect you even more. Now he knows you are wife material and it wasn't your fault that it ended so he can forgive that all together and actually has a sense of pride because he got the woman that another man tried to mess over. As humans we want things that others have already validated. That's the reason why there are comment sections and ratings under products and services because we want to know what others have to say about it. The same goes with an ex-husband. That other man has already said that you are worth marrying and all men respect that because men understand what it takes for a man to marry a woman. It takes a lot of guts and courage to do so and to be a woman that is worth the effort, says a lot. The key here is that you make it clear that your ex is your ex and he will not interfere with your next. That man needs to know that he is out of your life and that you are ready to move on with life.

Ex-husband with kids: This is a little touchier because it brings into play the baby daddy element that most men are afraid of. But it's not entirely the same because you had a real commitment with your ex-husband so therefore a man comes in knowing that it was legit and that the division of custody will be regulated and mandated by the courts. Hopefully this man you are dealing with has kids also so he will at least have some understanding of what this process is like and respect it. Some idiot men will give ultimatums that are just ridiculous, like telling a woman that if she wants to be with him she has to cut her kids off completely and it's all out of insecurities and immaturity. Sadly there are women that will do that to have a man. If a man gives you an ultimatum like that then you have to be able to tell him to go kick rocks with open-toed sandals on. Don't let a man come in your life who isn't willing to respect the structure and functionality of it. If he can't get with it then he needs to get going.

Bisexuality: I can tell you right away that a real man feels that he is all a woman needs and he will not be okay with sharing his woman with another person, not even a woman. A real man will not even entertain the thought of you being with another woman, but he will be more forgiving of you being with other women in your past than other men. Having women in your past doesn't feel as threatening to a man as other men because he knows other women don't have the tools he has and that their touch and love was totally different. Nor does he fear a woman coming and beating him up over you like he would if it were other men. If you have women and men in your past then you need to sit down, get coaching or counseling and really figure out what it is you want out of life and do so by figuring out who you are in life.

I will tell you that what you will attract is a freak. By freak I mean a very sexually adventurous man that has always fantasized about being with two women at once and he will want you to engage in threesomes. I can tell you this for sure; if a man asks you to have a threesome he is a **grown boy**. He does not really love himself nor does he really love you. You are expendable to him. It's like a coach being okay with you playing on his team and the opponent's team. If he does that then obviously he doesn't feel you are worth enough to want you all to himself nor does he see you or the other woman as a threat. I notice that the men who love threesomes and bisexual women are men who were not able to get girls while growing up through school and college—they were the guys that fantasized and watched porn on their laptop or dvd's and now they want to live out those fantasies. Again, I repeat, a real man will not want to share you with anyone else. A man who really loves you will want you to himself. Pimps share their women, not real men. And you know what a woman means to a pimp, not much at all. But to a real man you mean everything and he will want to be everything to you.

So if bisexuality is in your past it is forgivable to a man, although it may disturb him a little bit. He may also be paranoid that there is something a woman offers you that he cannot and that may scare him away when things begin to get really serious. If you want a man, then make sure you want a man and that you find a man who really loves you for who you are and not just for what you can do or are willing to do. Don't get caught up fulfilling a man's fantasy and being his pawn on the chessboard of life. Instead be his Queen! Be his everything! Do not compromise your self-worth and self-respect to be with a man. Don't allow a man to come into your life and be your "pimp." Make him respect you as a woman. But in order to do any of that you first have to know who you are and what you want out of life. Do not feel that a man deserves to have you and another woman at the same time and do not feel that you have to do that to keep a man because if that's what a man requires of you then he isn't a man worth keeping. Sleeping with him and other women to satisfy him will not quench his lust. Lust cannot be quenched like thirst. In fact the more you feed into it then the stronger it gets. So unless you want your man to up and walk out of your life one day, make sure you require that you are his one and only. If a man is what you want, then be with a man. If you want a man and a woman then that's a personal choice but I can tell you now that the odds are not good if you are seeking a happy and fulfilling life. I've coached way too many horror stories in that department to tell you otherwise. Love yourself first, and then a man will love you in return.

Compromising lines of work: The most common type of compromising work is stripping or exotic dancing. There are many guys who date strippers. There are also many strippers looking for a husband or at least a serious relationship. The problem with that is a man who is willing to be committed and faithful is very rare. Those guys have a lot of self-love and self-respect. Therefore, they are looking for a woman who loves and respects herself also. A stripper doesn't necessarily love and respect herself while in that profession. One may say she does love and respect herself, but that is only because she doesn't fully understand what it means. Dressing nice, taking showers, and not sleeping with every man that asks isn't the definition of loving and respecting yourself. Loving and respecting yourself would be to see your body as a temple and something sacred and wanting to save it for your husband. It would mean that you are a person with value and not a piece of meat on a showcase for a man to pick out and pay for to own a piece of your time or of your life. You are a human being and not an object. You are God's precious creation and not a man's means to make money by having you sliding down a pole. It's okay to love dance, but there is choreography, and dance teams, and dance competitions and things of that sort that can fulfill that passion and keep your self-respect in tact. There are other ways to make money than using your naked body to do so. Typically men see strippers as an object and not a person. Or they see strippers as a person who doesn't know their worth or has lost their way. Therefore it makes her vulnerable, gullible, and naïve to the ways of a man. A man feels that if she will get naked and dance in a crowded, dark, smoky club so that people can throw dollars at her then what wouldn't she do for money? That is not the light you want to be seen in as a woman.

Why do men date strippers? Strippers have a sex appeal that other women don't have. They have a sexual boldness or freedom that turns a **grown boy** on. Again it's usually men who did not have a lot of women or sex in his high school and adult years or a man who didn't have a solid upbringing and does not know what real love or a real relationship is. But usually it's a grown boy who wants to fulfill some fantasies. Also some strippers are the prettiest women who were abused at a young age by an older man and lost her innocence and lost her way. Therefore a **grown boy** with some fantasies will want her. As I think about the relationships I know of that consist of a man and a stripper they all are guys who were raised in a single parent home, they did not have girls flocking to them growing up in high school or early adult years, and they have no real moral sense or moral compass to go by. Therefore they are just as lost and confused about their identity as the stripper they are dating. I say that in all honesty and in the best way that I can say it. Therefore the argument from women who don't strip that all the men are dating strippers isn't true. The men aren't dating strippers, the **grown boys** are. The sad part to me is that this woman who strips is a good person with a heart! She is a human being who simply felt this was the best way to have a "good life" and make enough money to provide for herself and her kids if she has any. She maybe was abused or raped or molested as a young girl or simply raised with a slack hand. She is still a human with a heart. What hurts is that the men she attracts will not respect her. They will see her as a fun time, a means to an end, an experiment, but not their wife. You show me a happily married stripper; no show me at least six that you know of. You won't find it because real men who will be faithful and marry a woman are not interested in marrying a stripper. They will have a good time with one before marriage, but they won't marry her.

It hurts me that this is the truth. It hurts me that it has to be that way. But there is hope. A woman can grow. A woman can change. A woman can learn and she can attract a real man once she's become a real woman. Stripping is not the end all be all. Stripping is not the lowest form of life or the end of the world. Stripping is a phase of life. It's something some women go through and something that a woman should get through as fast as possible.

Can an ex-stripper find a husband? Yes! She can find a husband but she may have to be years removed from it so that she and the man can say that it was a phase in life and that it was a mistake and something she did when she was young and lost. If a woman is 35+

and still stripping then that presents a problem for a real man and the chances are very slim that a man will marry her before she is 40-45. If you are reading this and you are a stripper I want you to know that you are loved. If not by anyone you can pinpoint you are loved by God and you were created for more than stripping. You were created for a purpose and this just happens to be a part of your story. I ask that you look yourself in the mirror today and begin to love yourself. Decide to make more of your life than this and do something that the world will remember. It may be starting a foundation to help other strippers stop stripping and go to school. It may be writing a book. It may be working in a creative field like choreography. It may be a foundation for young girls so that they don't go down the same path you went down. Let your pain birth your purpose. Let your mess become your message. Let this be a stepping-stone and not a stumbling block. Change the way you see yourself and it will change the way you see the world and the way the world sees you. There are some young girls who only you will be able to reach. You'll be able to reach them because you've lived through this and now is the time to start walking in that purpose and living out your calling. This is not your calling; this is a distraction from your calling. Refuse to lose and go on and do great things!

Should a man know everything in your past? Ladies, we all have a past and it should be just that, the past! It is not important to tell a man everything about your past because I can assure you that 8 out of 10 men that you meet will not tell you everything in their past. Men never tell women exactly how many other women they've been with. If a man was once abusive or controlling, he won't tell. But oftentimes women tell a man too much thinking they will just put it all out there to be honest and not have any skeletons in the closet. Please realize that what he does not know will not hurt him. If you know that there is no way for him to find out about certain things and that these things will not come out unless you tell them, then leave it that way. He doesn't need to know everything. You are a good person with a heart and you deserve love. But because a man does not know you or care for you when he meets you he will judge you very strictly and sometimes even things that you had no control over will scare him away if you tell him. Unless this particular thing weighs heavily on your present then he does not need to know about your past. If he is snooping around and asking too many questions then call him on it. Ask him why it's relevant and make him give you a sound answer. Ask him those same questions before you answer and let your intuition tell you if he is being honest. Explain to him that your past is far removed from you and that you would not hold his past against him and he shouldn't hold yours against you. That is if you have some things in your past that you know he will be bothered by. If your past has five or less sexual partners in it and you are over the age of 21 then you have nothing to worry about. Anything over five and you could very well have some issues with that man. Just know that what you omit could come out one day and he still may leave you if he has an issue with it, so please make sure that is a chance you are willing to take. If it's not, then tell him up front and see if he will stay. If a man see's your heart and can feel that you are a good person and he is physically and emotionally attracted to you then he will forgive your past no matter what's in it. It does happen, but not very often. There are exceptions to every rule, but I don't want you to live your life trying to be the exception because you will get hurt in the process. The rules are the rules for a reason so understand that. Know that your past can affect you and if you already have a thick past then you need to start today by making better choices so that you are not adding to it. Save yourself, respect yourself, love yourself, prepare yourself, and position yourself because true love is on the way!

III
Why Is He Like That? Understanding the Man

*"Seek to understand then to be understood and you'll
spend less time explaining yourself."*

5

❧ *Understand a Man* ❧
but Remain a Lady

A woman can't think like a man and act like a lady because her thoughts will become her actions. Your thoughts become your actions and your actions become your life. So when a woman thinks like a man, she is crippling herself. The question is: how does a woman know how to think like a man? To do so will take away from her mind. Women have to understand the difference between a woman's thought process and a man's thought process. A woman's thought process is more complex than a man's. I think people took Steve Harvey's book title the wrong way. What he was saying is "understand the thought pattern of the opposite sex," but not to become just like the opposite sex.

In relationships: Women are able to not only listen, but also feel. Women seek to find solutions and are attentive to emotions, body language and tone of voice. Women are more talkative than men; the average woman speaks approximately 25,000 words a day. Men, on the other hand, only speak about 10,000 words a day and do not read emotions that are not verbalized. Men are more isolated where women are more open and friendly. That is why men-to-men friendships look very different than women-to-women friendships. These differences also explain why communication between men and women is often difficult.

The brain: Men process things better in the left hemisphere of the brain, but women are able to process equally in both hemispheres of the brain. This explains why men are more task-oriented and straight to the point, but women can tend to include emotions and feelings when solving problems.

Dealing with stress: Women handle stress better than men. It is in the DNA of a woman to do so. Men have a fight-or-flight response when it comes to stress, which is why we see so many men leave their families hanging when things get stressful, or you see the rare strong man who stands and fights. When it comes to women dealing with stress, Psychologist Shelley E. Taylor said it best: Women "tend and befriend." When things get stressful for women, they take care of themselves and their children (tend) and they form strong family bonds (befriend). These differences are part of the DNA of men and women. There is a chemical in our bodies called oxytocin, which is released in stressful situations in men and women. Women also produce estrogen, which enhances oxytocin and results in calm, poised, and nurturing feelings. This is part of the reason we see so many strong single moms. Men, on the other hand, produce testosterone, which decreases the effects of oxytocin; this is part of the reason why men run away from many stressful situations.

Dealing with pain: Men and women perceive pain differently because it is activated on different sides of the brain. In women, the left amygdala is activated, which is why women are better able to express that they are feeling pain and seek treatment. Men, however, internalize pain and may not let anyone know they are hurting. When men are hurting, even in a relationship, they may not say anything. Instead, they cheat. Women, on the other hand, will speak up about it and try to work it out. Even more than that, if they can't work it out, they either deal with it, cheat, or leave. Men usually just cheat until they find someone they like better than the women they're already with.

Emotions: Women are more in touch with their feelings because they have a larger deep limbic system, which allows them to make friends and bond with others more easily than men. Because of this ability to connect with others, women make better caregivers for children and others. The downside to women being emotional is that they can feel depressed when they have a hormonal shift, such as after childbirth or menstruation. Men don't feel as much, and when they do, they don't show it as much. Author Steven J. Dixon says, "Men don't heal, we ho," and that argument holds true in many cases.

Those are five differences in men and women, although there are many others that show why a woman shouldn't try to "think like a man."

A man isn't looking for another man unless he is homosexual, and even in those relationships, most don't act like "men;" at least one assumes the role of a woman typically. Heterosexual men are looking for a woman to complement them. If a woman is thinking like a man, she can't complement that man in a relationship. There will be many situations in a relationship where a woman's mind will be able to analyze in an effective manner, whereas a man's mind may fall short. Science shows that women use both sides of their brain, but men only use one side. Women can express emotion openly; however, men will pull back and look at everything logically, often without sympathy or empathy. A woman has so much that she brings to the table when she is in her purest form. A woman's genetic makeup allows her to be a mother and raise her family. Even in her sleep, she hears her child's cry in the middle of the night and attends to it. She can be passionate with her kids in a way that most men can't. A man, on the other hand, can lose control in a lot of stressful situations in the home. Therefore, a man needs a woman to be sound and stable. So, by keeping her own mind, she makes him a better man. She helps him grow and see life from a different perspective, which opens his eyes like never before. Her being herself helps him change.

As a husband, if my wife thought like a man, we wouldn't get anything done. If she thought like a man whenever I make her mad, she would just run out and cheat on me. If she thought like a man, then my son would miss a lot of the love and affection he needs. If she thought like a man then all we would ever do is argue; neither of us would ever be the bigger person to just walk away. But because she thinks like a woman, it's our differences, not our similarities that bring strength. She had the foresight to see beyond where I was to who I could be and she helped me get there. Because she was thinking like a woman, she put her foot down and demanded that I change and that I loved her back. I went from a grown boy to a grown man. If she had thought like a man, she wouldn't have cared where I was in my life and she would have just left. So please understand that there are many great benefits in thinking like a woman! God has given you that mindset on purpose; He knew that man would be unstable at times. He knew that man would be unfaithful at times. He knew that man would be unreliable at times. So He gave women strength and stability that helps their minds process situations in a way that strengthens them so that they are able to keep going in the worst of times. Women have a thought process that can keep them moving forward even when it seems that everything around them is going downhill; whereas men, in some of those same situations, may have thrown in the towel.

So ladies, I'm asking you to keep and cherish your mind because it is an asset to a relationship, not a liability. I don't really believe that Steve Harvey meant any harm when he used the title "Act Like a Lady, Think Like a Man," because this phrase was coined long before Steve's book ever came into existence. I believe that the person who started this phrase was someone who had been hurt time and time again by a man and said:

You know what? I'm going to try and beat a man at his own game. Instead of being naive and gullible or foolish, I'm going to beat them at their own game. I'm going to cheat when I want to cheat. I'm going to sleep with who I want to sleep with and I'm going to leave before I get left.

But being a woman and thinking like a woman does not mean being weak. Being a woman does not mean you are less than a man. Submissiveness is not stupidity. Submissiveness stems from stability and strength. Submissiveness is not a weakness. What women have to understand is that you can be strong-willed and still be a woman.

And thinking like a woman is to go above and beyond and out-think a man. Women must understand that they have all the power! Understand that if a woman told a man that he had to chop off one foot to get between her legs, he'd only have one foot. But where women go wrong is when they give in. They give up their power to a man because they feel like if they stand their ground, he will leave or he will stay and not love them. Women are more powerful than they understand because most men only want one thing and that's what is between a woman's legs. He will go to the end of the Earth to get that one thing! If more women would realize that power as a fact, there would be a lot more successful marriages in America. If women begin to demand that men give them a real commitment before they have sex, the world changes! A real commitment means a title, a ring and a wedding date. If marriage isn't the goal, then I don't know why you're dating.

It has nothing to do with just marriage itself, but a *healthy* marriage, and women have to understand every woman can achieve this goal by thinking like a woman. Don't disable yourself by thinking like a man. Men have done a lot of stupid things. A man thinking like a man, following his small head instead of his big head has gotten men in a lot of trouble. Presidents have ruined their legacies; husbands and fathers have ruined their families. Many men have passed fatal diseases from thinking with their "little head." So when a woman says she is going to start thinking like a man, she is essentially saying she is going to start thinking with a "little head" that she doesn't even have, and ignore the head on her shoulders. Now when you break it down like that, what is logical about thinking like a man? Can you even imagine how tragic that would be?

So I urge you ladies reading this chapter to think like a lady and act like a lady. But in order to think like a lady, you must first understand the power of your mind. You must first know your worth. A lady is strong! A lady is smart! A lady knows her worth. She knows never to compromise her self-respect. She knows what hand she holds and how much power she has. A lady understands that she is the spine of this world and that God put her in that position to be the Mother of this Earth. What's stronger than Mother Nature? Nothing! What's stronger than a woman? Nothing!

I'm not saying all of this to say what you want to hear. I'm saying this because this is what you *need* to hear. I'm not saying all of this to put down men! I'm saying all of this to lift up women and to verbalize what God intended from the beginning. When we see a woman in her purest form, we already know what she can accomplish. We've all seen the results of a strong woman who has embraced her beautiful mind. Then, on the other hand, we've seen the woman who has embraced the mindset of a man. Women who have embraced the mindset of men go from man to man seeking love but never find it because what they believe a man to be is actually the opposite. What they believe a man to be is actually a grown boy. So in essence, you're not emulating a man. You're emulating an immature adult male. You're emulating an idiot, and everything that you possess and everything you are, you've thrown out the window. So what you'll find yourself doing is going from relationship to relationship, going from man to man, sleeping with any- and everybody just because you feel some type of chemistry. You're telling yourself you're doing it because men are doing it too, but what you're not realizing is that when you fight fire with fire you'll only burn down the house. On the other hand, if you fight fire with water and handle a situation with the mindset of a lady, then you'll eventually extinguish that fire.

So instead of going from man to man, instead of leaving before you get left, instead of being hurt and hurting others out of vengeance, instead of lying, deceiving, cheating and trying to play people like a deck of cards, instead of doing all those things like a grown boy would, be a lady, be classy, and be respectful to yourself. Set an example for what type of woman you'd want your son to marry. Set an example for what type of woman you'd want your daughter to become. Set an example for what type of woman you'd want men to desire. I guarantee you when you realize your self-worth and when you commit to never compromising your self-respect, you will attract a real man and not a grown boy. You will attract real love and what so many of us think to be a fairytale will become your reality.

Please try to understand this and wrap your mind around this concept that a woman's mind is a very strong tool; to think like a lady is the very best thing you can do in your life and in a real relationship. Any real man will appreciate and respect your beautiful mind because he realizes that you're an asset and you increase his worth. He will realize that with you, there is nothing he can't do. Understand that and never let go of it.

Don't think like a man; just learn how to understand him. There is a difference between thinking like a man and understanding a man.

6

❧ *Getting Him to Express* ❧ *How He Really Feels*

B*e tough, boys don't cry!* Those very words have been echoed over and over throughout a boy's adolescence. It's those words that teach men to hold back what they are really feeling on the inside and to only cry when no one is looking. Because of that there have been some harmful side effects that usually effect interpersonal relationships with men. Men have been systematically programmed to shut down and to shut out. When things get too tough most men shut down. When a man feels like crying he is usually confronted with the fight or flight syndrome and he chooses one or the other. Because of this men have perfected the poker face in a relationship and are usually unable to express real feelings—good or bad. This is by no means standard for all men, but this is true for the vast majority of men. You can probably picture in your mind situations in grade school where there were two females who got into a screaming match and they screamed and pointed in each other's face for five minutes and nothing happened between them before it was broken up. Then on the other hand you can picture two guys who got mad at each other and they may have said two words before fists were flying. That is the difference between women and men. As you read earlier, there are scientific differences between women and men that effect how we communicate with one another. Men say what they mean and women understand what they wanted to hear. There is a big difference between to the two. A man can say "I don't feel like having sex right now," but a woman hears "I'm not attracted to you anymore so I don't want to sleep with you."

Women are very intuitive and use emotions in communication and are also sensitive to the emotions of others. Men, on the other hand are not so much that way. If a woman is talking to someone and the person starts to cry she will stop most likely. But a man will keep pouring it on until he is satisfied and has said what he has to say, no matter how many tears have been shed by the person he's scolding. If you analyze life you won't have to look very far to see that there is a very distinct difference between the way men and women communicate.

So, how do women get more out of a man? Men can speak and articulate themselves very well if given the opportunity. It just has to be on his time. The key to get more out of a man is to hear what he's not saying as well as what he is saying. Men will tell you they love you without saying, *I love you.* His actions will show it. He will hug you, he will caress you, and he will spend quality time with you. Then you have guys who will say I love you all day long but they don't touch you, spend much time with you, or seem to be fazed by much going on with you. Both guys are saying the same amount just in different ways. The bottom line is that actions speak louder than words. So I tell my female clients to pretend to be Helen Keller with a man and don't hear or see anything but only what the heart can feel. If your heart can't feel it then it's not real.

When it comes to arguments you have to be able to read his body language. A rule of thumb is that *the truth never gets offended.* What that means is that if a man is telling the truth there is no reason for him to get mad and try to flip the script or get verbally or physically abusive. That is a clear sign that he has been cornered and he is guilty. The truth does not coincide with anger; lies coincide with anger. The truth is calm, gentle, and sure of itself. The truth has no need of yelling, screaming, cursing, and obscene behavior—lies are tied to those things. If a man is telling the truth and you are pressing him about an issue he will laugh you off or just sigh and through up his hands. If he is lying then he will get angry and try to flip the script on you and make you feel guilty for even questioning him. Gary Chapman refers to it as manipulation by guilt. I'm not sure that it could be labeled any better than that. If I had to label it I'd call it the **reverse insanity plea,** which is where a man tries to get off the hook by making you feel like you're crazy. It's an age-old trick that works wonders and usually women will back off or let it go when a man does this. I've coached countless women who fell for this very thing. Ladies, trust your intuition because it is rarely, if ever wrong. It has never been wrong in judging me, but like most men, I was always able to talk a woman out of her intuition.

If you see a man getting hostile then let him know that you all will talk later but this is not over. Men do not respond well when they feel trapped or backed into a corner and he will either get violent or try to escape. Neither is the result you want because it only brushes the issue under the rug for you to trip over it later. It's okay to remove yourself from the argument and let things cool off and bring it up in a time of peace. If peace turns into war again then retreat again but let the man know that you will not keep coming back. If a man truly cares for you then he will muster up what it takes to articulate himself the way he needs to. If he doesn't really care for you he will simply say that he has said all that he's going to say and he's not saying anymore. If you are not satisfied with the answer you've received then you have to be bold enough to walk away from the argument and possibly from the relationship; especially if it is dealing with a major issue like infidelity or an outside child or any type of abuse.

The way a man carries himself and the way he expresses himself is a sign to you trying to teach you how he loves. If you want him to see how he loves then you have to mirror his image and treat him that very same way as long as it's not degrading to you and then if he questions why you are doing that then you have an opening. Tell him that you are simply doing what he does so you figured that he would understand it better since he does it so well. This is something that he will hear and process and he will make the necessary changes and begin loving you and expressing himself to you the way you need him to so that you will reciprocate. It worked perfectly when my wife did it to me.

Balance this information and know this does not mean to act like a man. What it means is if he doesn't call you then don't call him. If he doesn't show you affection then don't show him affection. That is the extent of it. It doesn't mean to go sleep with another man if he has slept with another woman. In that case you should leave him instead of hurting yourself or degrading yourself to get even. If you can't wrap your mind around that concept then you simply need to paint a picture with words for him so that he can put the shoe on the other foot and imagine how it would feel if you reciprocated his behavior. Contrary to popular belief men are not dense or dumb. Men are capable of real expression and real growth. It's just that sometimes, as a woman, you have to require that of him. Don't accept mediocrity in expression from a man. Instead push him to that next level and trust that he will go there. Communication is very important in a relationship and without proper communication the relationship will not work.

7

🎀 *The Man Who Earns* 🎀 *Less than You Do*

Sex and security: Two things men want in a relationship: sex and security. The two are closely related in the mind of a man. Sex is an expression for a man in good and bad ways. When a man is happy and secure he expresses it through sex. When a man is sad and insecure he expresses it through sex. Men want to be the one who brings security to a woman's life because for a man it is directly connected to his manhood and self-worth. For most men his self-worth is directly proportionate to his net-worth. The less he makes the more worthless he feels. If there are no rule makers then a man can deal with making less money, but if a man's rule maker is his woman and he makes less money then it becomes next to detrimental to his mental and emotional stability. Men define themselves by how much money they make and what they can give to a woman. The most common argument I hear amongst men who have not yet settled down is that they are not where they want to be financially. It's a common misconception that financial security will determine the success of the relationship, but it's almost become a rule because of the emphasis that our society puts on money and status. Therefore men, who make less than a woman, usually handle it in very toxic ways. The most common type of behavior will be a man who becomes very controlling, verbally abusive, inconsiderate, degrading, unfaithful, verbally and emotionally abusive and sometimes even physical. Men respond this way because they feel worthless and less than a man and these are simply coping mechanisms. It's like a young boy throwing a temper tantrum. It's the same thing except grown men won't stomp and cry or roll on the ground. Instead men start sleeping around looking for a woman to appreciate them or they try to debase the woman so that she feels less than him. He wants to be looked up to by her and have some type of power over her. It's a weakness in that man, not strength. He doesn't understand what true manhood is nor does he understand what real strength, power, or self-control is. When you recognize these behaviors in a man then you must leave him immediately because it will only get worse. As soon as he engages in any toxic behavior he begins to dig himself a hole and it only gets deeper and deeper. If you stay with him then you are reinforcing those behaviors and they will only repeat themselves. If you stop them by stepping away from the relationship then he will realize he has to change in order to have you. I believe in second chances but on that second chance he needs to get it right and keep it right and if he doesn't then you must leave him for good. He can grow, but not with you! That's just a hard cold truth! I see it every day so trust me. In that case you must let him go so he can grow! Not many men can handle a woman making more money than him because in his mind the man wears the pants and must be the breadwinner in the home. It's the way that our society has shaped us.

If you look at celebrity couples where the woman made more money than the man or had more power or influence than the man, the man usually ends up cheating on her. It's his way of coping. It's him saying since my woman doesn't respect and appreciate me I'll go to someone else who does. Therefore he is usually cheating down, meaning he's cheating with a woman that is easy, or makes less money than him. It's someone that makes him feel like more of a man in his mind and it's his way of getting back at his woman for making him feel the way he does. Even though it's not her fault at all, he can't see that in the moment.

How do I know if he can handle the fact that I make more money than him? As the good book says, *you will know the tree by the fruit it bears.* The same is true for a man. You will know by his actions. Signs that a man is safe, sound, and secure with you making more money than him…

- ✓ He will ask to support you
- ✓ He will join your team in a synergistic way, not in a cancerous way
- ✓ He won't try to change anything about you, only enhance it with your approval
- ✓ He will not be verbally, emotionally, or physically abusive
- ✓ He will have no signs of infidelity
- ✓ He will be inspired by you to become a better man and pursue his dreams
- ✓ He will not put restrictions on your endeavors
- ✓ He will not ask you to sacrifice any part of your life for his sake
- ✓ He will protect your assets and not exploit or abuse them

Finding this man will be no easy task at all. Mainly because of how society has brainwashed men, but slowly and surely more men are warming up to this idea because more women are ascending to greater heights in our society. It's important that when you meet a man you take it very slow and that you don't give him too much influence in your life too early. Many men take advantage of a woman's kindness and innate desire to be submissive to a man. A man will come in and become CEO of your brand and drive it right into the ground if you aren't careful. I've seen it done over and over. Some weak men will sabotage your business or career so that you have no choice but to be less than him and look up to him and let him be the sole provider for the home. It's sad but it's real and just like every other section in this book I must give you the cold, hard, truth. So make sure you thoroughly screen a man before you bring him into your life and even when you do, put him on a probationary period in your mind that he doesn't even know he is on. Then evaluate him every 3-6 months and do not be afraid to terminate him from your life if he is not performing, as a man should. Life is too precious to waste it on a bum of a man. Bring in a man that will be an asset and not a liability.

8

❦ *The Abusive Man* ❦

What is abuse? Abuse is any form of toxic behavior like…

- Cutting off your friends and family
- Choosing your clothes
- Choosing your outings
- Checking your phone
- Checking your email
- Checking your social media accounts
- Cursing at you
- Criticizing you all the time
- Cutting you down
- Manipulation
- Deception
- Pushing, shoving, hitting, smothering, restraining,

Abuse starts in ways that could be seen as cute or loving. It's a slight suggestion that you shouldn't go out any more and only stay in with him. It's as small as telling you that you can't wear certain types of clothes or hang out with certain friends. It's as small as telling you that you can't talk to your parents or family or friends as much on the phone or even see them in person as much. It starts very small and subtle and if you don't call it out then it only escalates.

Humans are selfish for the most part. On top of that true love isn't very common in our society. So we grow up seeing the seven deadly sins instead of true love. Love is a learned behavior and if we do not grow up seeing love exemplified in the home then we will not know how to express love to others. Men suffer from this just as well as women. Men are able to express their self-hate or inadequacy in different ways because men are the stronger of the two in a relationship. Therefore men can physically and mentally dominate a relationship most of the time. Men understand the effects of derogatory words when used against a woman. Therefore if a man has not been built up in his life and he doesn't know love or doesn't love himself then he will try to strip a woman bare of all self-worth and self-esteem. It's an attempt to have someone inferior to him so that he can feel some sense of worth or power in the world. He is a **grown boy** and just like little boys he needs a teddy bear, but being that he is grown up in stature he cannot carry around a teddy bear or sleep with one so he subconsciously tries to mold a human being into his human teddy bear. An object that he can abuse, and tear apart when he is down and hurting, and then he can pick up and put back together when he wants to cuddle at night. This is abuse and this is how it starts. If it is not recognized then it will escalate and only get worse. Most women don't recognize it because they too have never been taught real love and the dynamics of a real relationship just like that man. Therefore the two become a beautiful nightmare full of self-hate and low self-esteem but it's disguised as unconditional love. When it fact it isn't love at all. Then this so called love begins to bring pain to their life and the next thing you know this is where the slogan "love is pain" was birthed. Neither party knowing that love is the opposite of that and love has no parts of pain and is the furthest thing from pain. Love is then given a bad name and then the epidemic is spread across the world in a blink of an eye. Now, we find more toxic and painful relationships than we find healthy and wholesome ones. Pain is the enemy of love; they are not one in the same.

The women who become victims of self-hate are often those who have never been taught love from a man who really knew love. They are women who had to learn the hard way or figure it out on their own. Self-hate does not discriminate based on race, ethnicity, size, or gender. It will reside in whoever is willing to let it. Self-hate crosses all borders and territories and infiltrates the hearts and minds of the misinformed and unloved. It disguises itself as love and lies intertwined with some truth. Therefore it is rarely recognized before it's contracted and then spread around. The only way to stop it is to do what you are doing right now—be exposed to the truth and what real love is. Real love is not pain. Real love knows no pain. Real love is freedom, not captivity. Real love heals, not hurts. Real love cures, not infects. Real love is the solution, not the problem.

The women who fall outside of society's description of beautiful are often the ones that become targets of men filled with self-hate. He feels that you hate who you really are and because of his size, demeanor, or harsh words he can overpower you and make you his human teddy bear. He finds out that he can say a mean word to you once and you will let it cut you and then continue to cut you numerous times because you repeat it to yourself over and over and never let the wound heal. And because of his self-hate and inner pain if he sees you're beginning to heal then he re-opens the wound before it has time to fully heal. Then even when it does heal, it leaves you scarred, and if you accept his cruel words then eventually it will become his cruel hands. One form of abuse leads to another, but no form of abuse is any less dangerous than the others.

What you must understand is that love should not hurt you, love should not trap you, and love should not have you in tears. Love should lift you up and make you feel good. Love is not a fairy tale, it is a reality and I know it's real because I'm living it. I've been in an abusive toxic relationship. I've been the abuser and I've been abused. Remember there are many forms of abuse; it's much more than just physical. Now I'm in a loving relationship where there are no more tears, no more fights, no more painful nights, but everyday is another day to grow and get better. There are disagreements but they do not turn violent or abusive because love always prevails. Once you know and experience real love you will never settle for less. If you are in an abusive relationship then the best and the only option for you is to leave! Start fresh and new. Enter into a relationship with love and friendship as the foundation instead of lust, lies, and deception. Once a man begins to communicate with you in an abusive way he may never stop. There is a chance that he will always revert back to those abusive ways if you don't leave him and let him learn what real love and a real relationship is supposed to be like. Do not be fooled into believing that love is pain and that love must have chaos just because he says so or has shown you so. But believe what I'm telling you because I'm living on the other side. You can and you will find real love if you accept nothing less!

Why do men abuse? There are many reasons why, but the biggest reason that people often over look is that this behavior is innate in all humans, but many learn how to reject these feelings and respond to situations instead of react. How is it innate? Do you remember when Cain got jealous of Abel and he killed him? That was the second generation of the world and hate and violence had already showed its ugly face. Since then we have been born into that same vain and then we learn how to behave and how to control ourselves. Think over the events in your life and see if you can remember a time that you were so angry you cursed someone out or called them a name or slapped or punched someone. Can you remember it? I'm sure you can unless you're an angel. Men and women alike have abused someone in some way whether it was verbal, emotional, or physical. It could have been a friend, a family member, your child or your spouse. It's innate. It's a natural reaction when we get upset or hurt. As they say, *hurt people hurt people.* But when it happens to us we forget that it is human nature and we label that person a monster. They aren't monsters, they are hurting, they've been abused, they are suffering on the inside and they need someone to see that and stop them before they self-destruct. Men abuse for the same reasons women abuse. Whether it's a natural reaction or it's a learned behavior, it's an expression of pain and a cry for help.

How can you help? What you don't want to do is hurt yourself by trying to help. Staying with an abusive partner is not helping them it's hurting them. What can help is speaking into their life at a time of peace. Tell them that they are worth more than that and that you know they are a better person than that. Help them identify their gifts and their purpose for those gifts. Tell them what you see them being able to do in the world. Let them hear words of affirmation that they've never heard before. Most of the time they are hurting because they've never been affirmed. They've never had anyone believe in them as a human being and as a productive citizen in our society. They need that. It doesn't have to be at your expense. If a person is abusive and can't seem to stop you must call for help, a Pastor, the police, a life coach, someone. They have to know that you are not afraid of them and that you do have back up and resources behind you. Do not fear leaving them because to stay is much more dangerous than to leave. Your presence will be reinforcing the behavior and it will only make it worse. Be bold enough to leave. You may have to wait until a time of peace to leave, but make sure you leave. Do not go back; let them go so they can grow! I can speak on this because I lived through it. I left a very toxic relationship where abuse of all sorts was present. Had I stayed one of us would have killed the other or ourselves. I'm not speaking from a book I've read like some, I'm speaking from real life experience. I know some of you reading this have lived through it also, please speak out about it and help others. Abuse is a taboo subject and many are afraid to speak on it because it might be happening in their own home. Do you notice that there is a reality show on everything but abuse? I tried to produce a show on abusers and helping them change and the production companies and networks told me that it was too dark of a subject to talk about. The media will only let doctors speak on it but little do they know that those very doctors could be abusing their partner or being abused! Again, I'm not just speaking about physical abuse. I am speaking about all kinds of abuse. None of it is acceptable and none of it should be tolerated! If you are going through it then get out of it. If you know someone going through it then help them get out of it even if they don't want help, call the police for them. There is only one of two results of abuse if a person is unwilling to leave and that is prison or the grave. Let's stop abuse!

9

🎍 *Why Some Men Cheat* 🎍

"**A** person doesn't cheat because something is wrong with you. They cheat because something is wrong with them."

To put it simply, a man cheats because he doesn't know if the woman he is with is the woman he wants to be with for the rest of his life. Men are visual creatures. Men are sexual creatures by nature. One of the first charges given to man was to be fruitful and replenish the Earth and because of the massive population that needed to be created, man was made in a special way with a sexual appetite that can rarely be put into words. Now we have a law that a man can only be married to one woman and infidelity is against the law in the minds of the people. The problem is the genetic make-up of man has not changed; only the laws have changed. The hearts and minds of men have not changed, only the laws have changed. Therefore the Kings that had 1,000 wives had the same body parts and hormones that the men today with one wife have. What is the difference between the two? Nothing but the laws we live under. That is where the problem comes in. Until men learn to condition their hearts and minds to be set on something else other than women then infidelity will always be an issue. That's on the biological side of cheating, but there are other reasons why.

Another reason men cheat is because they are looking for an upgrade. Just like with phones, cars, and clothes, men sometimes classify women the same way and he always wants the latest and greatest. The grass always looks greener on the other side but he is not realizing it looks that way only because he's not watering the grass he has. Men will risk their heart to have some legs, not realizing that it's the heart that gives life not the legs. What that means is that men will risk a perfectly fine relationship for a nice set of legs walking by. This has been the downfall of a many great men and will forever be that way. There will be a select few that step out of the line of dominoes and break the curse but those men are few and far in between at the moment, but I'm hoping to lead a change in that area.

Another reason men cheat is to retaliate. Men are big babies sometimes and cheating is a form of a temper tantrum. Since a grown man can't scream, yell, cry, stomp, or roll on the ground, he cheats. He cheats to try and hide his pain, or insecurities. He is confusing pleasure with happiness and not realizing that pleasure does not lead to happiness, but pleasure leads to pain. He doesn't realize that the two minutes of pleasure will lead to an STD, an illegitimate child, a breakup, a divorce, a fight, and a bad case of karma. He isn't processing those things; he's just caught up in the pleasure of the moment. As they say, *ignorance is bliss.* Ignorance is bliss until the consequences hit and then he is given the space to either learn and grow from it or continue down the same wretched path.

Contrary to popular belief, once a cheater does not mean always a cheater. Men can change! This I know because I'm a changed man. I used to cheat all the time on every woman I dated. I did it because I didn't know if the one I was with was the one I wanted to stay with but I didn't want to leave her until I found her replacement because I didn't want to be alone. I've come to find out as a Relationship Coach that many men have that same problem I once had. What stopped me from cheating? I believe in the Holy Bible now like never before. I read it and found in it that there are many principles and if we live by those principles there are promises and rewards. One of the principles is that we should live holy and pure without fornication and adultery, and the other sins we know about like greed, envy, lust, lies, murder, theft, idolatry and so on. I started living by those rules and then I began to reap the rewards. Because I began at a young age to experience God and how real this was I was sold on it. I know that if his blessings are real then his wrath must be real too. I started looking at people who claimed to live it but really weren't and something horrible would happen to them. I knew it to be real because those same types of things happened in the Holy Bible. Being a wise man as I consider myself to be I would not be a fool and fall victim to the wrath of God by living outside of His will. I keep the rules near and dear to my heart and I reap the rewards. The Holy Bible tells me that if I keep God's word and I live by it then anything I ask in His name will be granted unto me. I asked God for wisdom and He granted it. I asked God to show me my purpose and He showed me my gifts and and pressed on my heart to give them to the world. I travel the country and speak into the lives of others. God gives me visions and ideas and then the provision to bring them to life. These books, audio, apps, online schools, etc help change peoples lives and I know it's none of me but all of God. So because I found my purpose and I found God and I know them both to be alive and real, I walk inside of the confines of my faith and that is Christianity. Because of that, I am faithful to my wife because the Holy Bible demands it of me. My wife cannot hurt me, nor does she scare me, nor is she perfect. But more so than me being faithful to her I am faithful to the God that made me because it's Him who holds my fate in His hand, not my wife. I love her and that helps me remain faithful but our love for another human is not enough, as men we must fear something bigger than us and for me it's God.

To be honest, I believe there are other faithful men in the world because I know I'm faithful at this point in my life so I know there has to be others. I've had men tell me they are faithful but only them and God knows if that's the truth.If I can look at a man's life and see balance and stability with a strong set of morals then I can believe that he is living faithfully to his woman. What I'd say to women when it comes to a man cheating is that you should not worry about whether he will or not. Instead know who you are and what you are worth and know that if he does it's his loss and not yours. Love him with everything you've got and do all you can to keep him happy and require the same of him. You have to love yourself enough that even if he does slip up you can either forgive him & forget about it or you can walk away and not look back. If you truly love yourself although it will hurt you will be able to recover from it.

There are three things that I teach women to do to help prevent a man from cheating.

1) **Respect Self:** what this means is that you must let this man know that your life does not revolve around him and that you were fine before him and you will be fine after him. Do not let

a man curse you, disrespect you, use or abuse you. If he does any of those things you must put him in his place and step away and give it a break whether it's a day or a week or a month. It all depends on the severity of the offense. If you respect yourself then he will in turn respect you and that helps a man remain faithful because he knows that if you will take steps away from him for small things like cursing at you then there isn't a doubt in his mind that you will leave him if you catch him cheating.

2) **Remain Unpredictable:** what this means is that you must always stay on top of your game. If you get complacent you will get replaced. You have to update, refresh, and renew. You have to always be the latest and the greatest. What you won't do another woman will. So always stay on top of your weight, your fashion, your sex life, and so on. Do not get lulled into thinking that he is yours and that he is never going anywhere. You will have a rude awakening and it will be heart breaking.

3) **Occupy Time:** what this means is that you must know his schedule and make sure that his free time is spent with you. You don't have to completely smother him but don't give him too much idle time. Don't get so caught up in yourself and your life that you leave him hanging or give him way too much freedom. Men are sexual creatures and will wander right into another woman's panties if you don't stay on top of his time. Mature men don't need more than one guy's night a week. If he needs more than one guys night a week then you may want to figure out if it's his boys that he's hanging with

or if there is another woman. A man who loves you will not mind spending time with you!

Those are three things that my wife has mastered and I must admit that although I have a very strong moral sense about myself her mastering those things really help me. Because even though I fear God we cheat on God everyday in some way, so that is not a sure fire way to stay faithful. But that combined with my wife doing those three things is enough to keep a major ex-womanizer like myself faithful. So that is a proven method.

To limit the chances of being cheated on make sure you choose a man that is put together. What I mean by that is that you should be able to look at him and talk to him and get a sense of where his head is. Does he know who he is? Does he understand what purpose is? Does he have concrete goals with a concrete plan? Is he full of ambition? What does his relationship resume look like? How many kids does he have if any? What is his lifestyle like? Is he living a life closer to a player or a pastor? All these things will give you a glimpse into who this man is and how he will be inside of a relationship with you. The more adventurous and daring a man is the more likely he will cheat. I say that because sex is one of the easiest things for a man to do. There are many men who will sleep with a woman unprotected before he would drink alcohol, get a tattoo, smoke weed, etc. Why? Because sex is easy to do! It's already in a man's nature and it doesn't take much thought. So if a man is living like a "bad boy" then you can bet your bottom dollar you are going to get cheated on, there are no doubts about it and I will bet my bank account and my son's college tuition on that. It does not fail!! To be faithful is one of the hardest things a man will ever do in his life and in order to be able to do that means he has all the other aspects of his life in order. I've been studying relationships and human behavior since the 9th grade. I've been coaching women on relationships since the 9th grade also. I also lost my virginity in the 9th grade. It's safe to say the 9th grade was the start of a lot of things for me. Through all those years of studying here are some things that I've found out about cheating…

- If he doesn't have a strong moral sense or faith -> he'll cheat
- If he's sexually active -> he'll cheat
- If he smokes, gets drunk, and parties -> he'll cheat
- If he loves porn-> he'll cheat
- If he loves the strip club-> he'll cheat
- If getting women is new to him-> he'll cheat

I don't want to generalize but those are some common denominators among men who cheat. I know two men who I believe in my heart are faithful, both are devout Christians, neither has tattoos, neither have gold teeth, neither drink, smoke, curse, both are part of the in-crowd, both are professional athletes, and both are saving themselves until marriage. Myself as a faithful man, I'm a devout Christian, I don't drink, smoke, curse, club, watch porn, gamble, or get any more tattoos, oh I don't have guys night out either. I do conduct business, may have guys come over to my house or have house gatherings, go on dates with my family or just with my wife. I travel the country alone a lot, but I don't hang out or get into anything. I do business and go back home. I say that to say when a man finds balance and stability in life is when he is most able to be faithful to a woman. That is what you want to look for and that is what you want to wait on. If a man's life is out of whack then his love will be out of whack too. If a man's morals are out of line then he will be out of line too. If he's breaking laws or doing illegal things then it'll be just that much easier for him to cheat.

I do not say these things to paint a very bad picture. I say these things to let you know how the man you are with or thinking about being with stacks up with my years of study. I'm twenty-seven, the other two men I mentioned to you are twenty-five, so that shows that it doesn't necessarily take a man forever to man up and settle down. You just have to wait on the right one. Be patient. You can't say, *well I curse and drink and smoke and club but I'd never cheat.* That is not valid because you are not designed like a man; what God put in a man he didn't put in a woman. Sex isn't as easy an act for a woman as it is for a man. Therefore a woman can drink, curse, smoke and not sleep around because it means more to her than those othere things that may be harmful to her mind and body. Men on the otherhand are designed differently and it's easier to have sex with a woman than it is to cure drinking and smoking. There are many men who do none of those things but yet they cheat on their woman. Why? Because sex is first nature for a man so it's safe to say that if a man's morals are out of wack then his sex life will be also.

Yes women cheat but not as much and not as easy as men. The women who cheat have been scorned and torn long ago and are now adapting to what they feel is the norm and what they feel is right. They feel that they would rather do it than have it done to them or that since a man is doing it then they should too. Never accept that mentality because you will only hurt yourself! That man can go on and find love because there will be a woman that accepts him but the same may not be true for you with another man. So don't stoop to a man's level. Don't do something that can eventually hurt you just because men are doing it. Don't adapt to the way men play the game, but instead stay steadfast in what you know is right and wait until a man is ready to elevate to your level.

There are faithful men, I'm sure of it. I just haven't met all of them nor will I. But I do understand the general make up of a faithful man and it's not rocket science. His life must be in order and he must be balanced and stable mentally and emotionally. Don't rush into love, take your time and let it come naturally!

10

❧ *Why Some Men Find* ❧ *it Easy to Leave a Woman*

From the moment a man sees a woman he makes up in his mind what role he thinks she will play in his life. He may not always be right but most of the time he is. He's right because he decides from the beginning what he wants her to be and unless she shows him otherwise, things will not change. When I first saw may wife in the mall selling jewelry I told myself that she would be a cute one night stand or just a cute girl I could have as a back up. But after one 6-hour conversation with her on the first day we met up to talk I had decided that she would be my wife. She showed me that she wasn't who I thought she would be, she was much more. I fell in love with what she showed me that day. I wasn't ready for marriage and neither was she but we were sure going to work towards it. Most men hate to be alone! But there are many men who are just fine alone. For the type of man that leaves a relationship easily, he is normally one of the ones who hate being alone. So, he finds a "**hold me down**" which is a woman he knows won't be his wife but he will date her, sleep with her, and even call her his girlfriend, but she is there to earn his love. It's not right but it's real! He is with this woman because he wants to be able to have sex on demand. He is a grown boy and he needs a human teddy bear. He gets a kick out of the drama that ensues in a relationship. He is always on top and always wins because he cares the least, while the woman is going through hell because she doesn't know that she's the "**hold me down.**" She thinks that this is serious and that they are really moving towards something real, but he knew from day one that she wasn't what he wanted in a relationship but he would do for the time being.

The irony in this is that several times while this man is trying to play this woman, he ends up playing himself. Either she grows on him or he falls for a woman that he never thought he would. Or she out grows him and leaves him hanging and now his ego is so hurt that he's chasing her when he expected it to be the other way around. I think all women who think they could be the **hold me down** because a man's heart doesn't really seem in it, should leave him. Leave him and see if he will come after you and if he does and you take him back don't give him any more than he gives you. If he doesn't get mad or seem to care then you have to take your heart out of it too. Be his mirror image and reciprocate what he gives you as I stated in an earlier section of the book. Again don't confuse it with acting like a man or thinking like a man; you just aren't giving more to the relationship than he is. Don't' degrade yourself under any circumstances. If you don't understand this then please sign up for coaching with me and I'll break it down and show you how it works. Listen to your intuition and don't allow yourself to get played. A man who cares about you will have an emotionally vested interest in you. He will put his heart into it and you will be able to tell that he cares about what happens in the relationship.

The reason men in these situations are able to leave so easy is because they aren't vested in it. Just like at a company, if you aren't vested in the company you'll leave much easier than you would if you were. You have to test his love to see if he's in it or if he's just biding time. If I could use another metaphor I want you to think about that car you got just to get from point A to point B. You told yourself that this is just temporary and when I get some money saved up I'm going to get a better car. Men are telling themselves the same thing about that woman that he plans on leaving. He's saying I'm going to be with her just so I don't have to sleep alone and so I can have someone to cook for me, clean for me, have sex with me, and cuddle me when I need her to. That's why as a woman you have to separate the benefits of marriage from the benefits of dating so that you don't get played like this. If you don't give a man all the benefits of marriage then he will leave you right away if he isn't in it for you. But if you give him all the benefits of marriage then why would he leave before he finds something better. So he rides you until it's about to fall apart and then he "upgrades" to someone else. I tell the women I coach, don't be a man's 'crash test dummy.' Don't let him test you out and wear you out and then just leave you hanging. Instead proportion the relationship and let him know that there are different stages to a relationship. In dating you do just that, date! In a relationship you do just that, relate! In an engagement you do just that, engage! In a marriage you do just that, live like a married couple where all the benefits are available to one another. The women who get played are the ones who give a man the benefits of marriage while dating. You give a man something he doesn't deserve yet nor has he earned, he takes it, you get worn down, and then he leaves you and now you are torn and scorned for your real love which is yet to come. But because you bought this book you won't have to go through that again if you already have and if you haven't then you are even more fortunate.

If a man left you and didn't look back please understand that he never intended on being with you. A man doesn't let go of something he really wants. That's why you see men in their mid 30's still chasing dreams from high school. Men do not let go easy at all if it's something that he really wants. So a man that left a relationship easy it's only because he went in to it knowing that this would be a phase in his life, a **hold me down.** He had no intentions of anything more real than that.

How do you stop that? You stop by not giving a man your all until he has given you his all. Just like it's a man's job to get on one knee, it's a man's job to lead. When I say lead by example I mean, the man should say, "I love you" first. The man should be the one to show you love first and then you reciprocate. The man should lay down his ego and his selfish needs and open up to you. When he does that then you can give him a little bit of yourself. Make sure what the man is giving you is really giving of himself. Money and gifts is not giving of him. His time and his title are giving of himself. At the end of the day if he gives nothing that impresses you or moves you then you shouldn't give him those things either. Don't go in working like a slave to win his heart because you are a Queen. It's his job to work for your heart. If you give to a man before he gives to you then a man will get complacent. But if you let him lead by example and let him give and then you reciprocate by showing love of your own then he will appreciate.

If he wants to leave then let him leave because holding onto someone that is trying to let you go will only get you hurt. If he has already left and you are wondering why, please understand that you didn't lose someone who loved you; you lost someone who lusted after you. Now change your outlook on yourself and this life, become love, and **prepare and position yourself** to attract real love.

IV
The Dating Game

"Everything comes full circle. Be careful what you send out because it's coming back around."

11

❀ Sex Before Marriage ❀ Can Hurt You

I get it! We live in a new day and age. We live in a very sexually charged society. Sex sells! Sex is everything these days. One-night stands are common now. Casual sex is common now. Friends with benefits are common now. Sex with no strings attached is common now. There are even box office hits about these very things. It's all sending a message, but it's all lies. It's contrary to what a sound relationship is made of. A sound relationship is not built on sex because sex is based on lust and to build a relationship on lust is like building your house on sand. A relationship must be built on friendship and friendship turns into love and there the foundation of successful relationships is love and friendship not lust and sex. In a real relationship where there is real love you will find out that sex is not a priority, it's a plus. That's how you have couples where they are old and still getting along just fine and has been married for decades. That's because they were friends before they became lovers and sex partners. Now, you have relationships built on lust and they don't even last five years, so a lifetime is way too far out of the equation.

I've found that mature men who are ready for marriage are looking for a lover not a **bump buddy.** A man who is serious and ready will wait for marriage to have sex because it's not about the sex; it's about finding a lifelong partner to spend the rest of his days with. I know men like this so I know they exist. These mature men understand that sex is all the same and that it all works the same and it all feels the same. The only difference between the feeling for a man is if there is any love in it. If there is no love in it then one woman is no different than the next. One may know more tricks than the other but at the end of the day it's a moment of pleasure, not true happiness. Love is what brings happiness.

In this day and time many women believe that if they don't have sex with a man that he will leave for another woman. That may be true but that means he didn't see you as his potential wife to begin with. I can promise you my left hand (I'm left handed) that a man WILL NOT leave a woman that he feels he can marry just because she wants to wait until marriage. If he does he's a **grown boy**, not a man. Therefore since women believe that lie they are giving in very fast and the man ends up wearing them out then running off with a piece of their innocence. Then after going through this every three months or every month a woman ends up with four to twelve sexual partners a year, and then from the age of 18-30 she's living this lifestyle and so when she meets the man of her dreams at thirty-one he doesn't want to touch her with a ten-foot pole. Although he will sleep with her like the other guys, because he's heard about her past or knows of her past personally he has taken her off his potential wife list. That sucks! Is it fair? No. Is it real? Yes!

So I want to let women in on a secret and that is that you can save yourself until you meet the man you know you can marry and then even with him you can make him wait and if his feelings are mutual HE WILL WAIT!! Please trust me on this. I know because I was once a very promiscuous man and if I will wait I know average men with average sex drives will wait also. I coach and deal with several men so I have the inside scoop and I wouldn't lie to you about this. If you do it this way, at the end of the day if a man leaves you then you have lost nothing! But if you don't listen and you sleep with the guy and he leaves you then you've added another guy to your list and got no reward for it.

There is a thing in dating that I call the **full court press.** It's a basketball term and it works the same in dating. A man puts all the pressure on you about sex and he throws everything at you that he can trying to break you down and make you turn over the innocence so that he can "score." To stick with the metaphor, if you break down and you turn it over he scores and he wins. If you tough it out and you break the **full court press** then you score. His scoring relates to him having sex with you and then being able to move on and you've lost. Your scoring is winning his respect and possibly his heart and even if you don't then you've lost nothing. Is it fair that he's putting this **full court press** on you? No. Is it real? Yes! So ladies knowing this, I need you to break the press. If he doesn't like it, then tell him he can get to stepping because it's your ball and it's your rules. But if you don't break the press then you lose. I put the **full court press** on my wife and she kicked me out of her apartment! She won my respect that night and she turned out to be my wife. Guess what? She was the ONLY woman in my lifetime that I saw potential in and broke the **full court press** and look at the reward she got. She won a life long partner. All the other women that I saw potential in, they couldn't break the press so as a man we assume that if you gave it up to us then you most likely give it up to every other guy that pressures you too. Remember we don't really have big egos it's all a front. So we don't flatter ourselves and feel like it's something so special about us that made you turn it over. We feel like if you did it for us then you did it for several other men too. This is why sex before marriage can hurt you because it's a man's way of testing you to see if you know your own worth and if you will require that from a man. I've spoken with countless men who have confirmed this very mentality. Sure enough when you ask your male friend or boyfriend or man in your life there is a strong possibility he will say, *that's just his opinion he can't speak for all men.* I'm already calling it because that's what we all say when we know another man is right about something and it will make him look better than us or mess up what we are trying to do. So instead of running to a man and using this as a conversation piece, do your own research. Look back over your life at the men you've slept with within 12 months of daily interaction with him by phone or in person and count how many put a ring on your finger and married you. If you are a virgin then look around at some females you know and ask one how many men they've been with that they slept with in under 12 months and then ask how many of them married her; if she isn't lying then the numbers won't lie either. Sex will not keep a man; if anything if you give in too early it will be the fastest thing to push him away.

Men love the chase! Men love the hunt. So make a man work for you! If he has to work really hard for you when he gets you he will appreciate you. Giving in to sex in less than six months is too soon and if you can make it six months then make it a year. Every guy I talk to who used to be a womanizer but is now engaged or married, responds the same way whenever I ask them what made their partner so special. One of the first things they mention is how long she made him wait. I've spoken to countless numbers of men about it, but the two most recent are very good NBA players and you know the rap they get for sleeping around. I already knew the answer but for the people's sake I ask around and do polls just for the people who say, *you're just one person.* Oh, shut it up why don't you?! So what was confirmed is that men appreciate and respect a woman that makes him wait and makes him work for her heart! It can really change a man. Making a man wait is like dog training. You can literally turn a "dog" into a man, just by making him wait, and make him court you for your love.

So please, don't be thirsty! Don't be vulnerable and naïve. Don't be desperate for love! Desperation is a weak emotion and it produces weak results. Instead stand firm in your beliefs and know your worth. Love yourself and respect yourself. Make a man work for you and forget what other people are doing around you and go with what works. What's the worst that can happen if you don't give in to sex? He will leave you alone! And if he does, so what, that just means he wasn't meant to be there with you anyway. Anything worth having is worth waiting for and worth working for; we know that to be a fact. Well the same goes for you! You are worth the wait, so make him work!!

A woman who knows her worth understands that for her heart it is of the essence that a man has to WORK! ~Tony Gaskins Jr.

12

❧ Signs You're Moving ❧ Backwards, Not Forward

If you have been in a relationship for more than three years and you are having sex, living together, over the age of twenty-five, or have kids together and you do not have a real commitment then you are moving backwards not forward. I know not everyone believes in marriage and I can't force you to if you don't. I just believe a woman would be crazy not to make a man give her a legally binding commitment that puts parameters around the relationship and has rules and guidelines. It also provides some security and assurance that a man can't just up and leave. He has to plan it out, then pay money and go through a whole process to get out of it. That way you know if he goes through all of that, he is serious and deserves to be let out of it. Anything less than marriage is like doing business without a contract, having sex without a condom, working a job without benefits, speeding on a busy highway without a seat belt. I hope you get the picture. If marriage and a life long commitment isn't the goal then why even be in a relationship? What do you have to show for it when he decides he's tired of you after ten years? After you've become accustomed to this lifestyle and stability and now he wants to move on? It's just not smart to operate like that and that is exactly why God created marriage and the government created alimony, and things of that nature. Just think about it please. Back to what I was saying in the beginning, if you are experiencing any of those things or a combination of any of them then that is a sign that you are moving backwards. The last thing you want to do is move backwards! A man should know by twelve months if he wants to commit to you for good, and truthfully a mature man with a good head on his shoulders will know way before then. As I stated earlier I knew from the very first extended conversation that I wanted to marry my wife. When we got back together after our little split up in the very beginning, ten months later we were getting married. I knew it from the gate that I could marry her. Real men know what they are looking for just like you know what you are looking for. There is no excuse for a man to be with you for years on top of years and still haven't made a commitment. Unless you are his **"hold me down"** and you don't know it yet.

If you are living together and you have been living together for over two years and you are cooking, cleaning, having sex, and doing all the things that a married couple does and are not married then you are moving backwards, not forward. In that case you are giving a man all of the benefits of marriage but you do not have the assurance that he feels like you are wife material. That's not fair to you, nor is it smart of you to be in it. If you give a man all of the benefits of marriage without requiring that he muster up the courage to marry you then you take away the incentive of him ever wanting to marry you. If he can have all that a married man has but not have to share his last name or be bound by law from infidelity (not that it will stop him from cheating) then why would he want to get married? You see in marriage if he cheats and you decide to leave then you can get alimony at least or if he has some money to split you can at least walk away with a settlement or something for you trouble and move on with your life. I'm sure women who were cheated on horribly feel much better leaving with half of everything than empty handed. But if you are giving him the benefits of marriage, but you aren't actually married and he cheats and you decide to leave then you just have to pack up and leave empty handed. That's a fantasy for a grown boy. A grown boy fantasizes and drools at the mouth when he thinks of the possibility of finding a woman that has bought into this whole anti-marriage movement. He would love that because in the mind of a man if he isn't married then it's still open season. If he isn't married then he's technically still allowed to play the field. You can be replaced at any moment regardless of what his mouth says to you during pillow talk or foreplay. Don't fall for the okie-doke. I see this everyday and frankly I'm tired of wasting my breath coaching so many women who have been fooled by this. It's not smart. Stop moving backwards and start moving forward!!

13

❦ *Getting from* ❦ *Dating to Marriage*

There comes a time when you are tired of being the girlfriend or "fiancé" and now you are ready to be the wife! I hear it all the time. There's a woman who has been dating this guy for years now and they are having sex and he's whispering sweet nothings and talking about a baby and so on, but deep down in her heart she wants a commitment. She doesn't want to be a baby momma or end up a single mom without security because all of a sudden he bumps his head and decides he wants to leave. There is an issue at hand though, they are having sex already and she doesn't know what more she can do to make him want to marry her.

Here is the solution. It's not that you should do more because you've done enough, what you have to do now is do less. You have to take away his benefits package! If he wants to just be in a relationship then give him a relationship! Do you know what a relationship consists of? It doesn't involve living together! It doesn't involve you cooking, cleaning, and doing laundry for him. It doesn't involve you having his baby. It doesn't even involve marriage! All it involves is him picking you up and taking you on dates, paying for the food and then dropping you off at your place and then going to his place. He can call, he can text. He has no say so in your life and he cannot impose his will on you. Meaning he can't just show up at your job, classroom or home unannounced or without your permission. He can't tell you where to go, who you should and shouldn't hang out with and what you should and shouldn't be wearing. You all are basically exclusive friends that are allowed to peck on the lips and hold hands in public and go on dates. This is where the stuff hits the fan. He will kick, yell and scream, figuratively speaking. He will try to ice you out and not call you or speak to you for weeks if he can handle it. He will call your bluff! He will even cry if he needs to. If you do not give in to any of his attempts to have his way or impose his will or coerce you back into the mess hole you were just in then he will do one of two things. He will step up in your life and give you a real commitment. That means if you all are in a relationship he will propose and he is to be made aware that the wedding date must be set within a year. Otherwise you will be a fiancé for five years and still may not become his wife. Or he will step out of your life. Meaning he will break up with you. This is what you want to happen. You want to make him step up in your life or step out of your life. You shouldn't be doing this before one year is up. You can't pull this at three months, six months, or nine months. You all have had to be seriously dating for at least twelve months. Seriously dating means that you are a couple, people know you are a couple and you talk everyday like a real couple does. If that is the case then it would be smart to make this move after twelve months have passed if he isn't showing any signs of wanting to move forward.

I have had several women who did this and they got their man to take them serious and know that they meant business and they moved forward. One gentleman proposed in two weeks after she made this move on him. If he cares for you and really wants to be with you then he will make a move because he won't want to lose you. If he leaves you then you know he wasn't the one. Or he may ask for more time, and that is cool. It's perfectly fine to give him more time just let him know that it can't be the same way that it once was and that you all will have to cut out the sex and so on as stated earlier.

If he leaves you, do not chase him or beg him back because then you will have lost all of his respect and he will know that you are just a bluffer. So even if you have to reach out to me to have me hold you accountable and coach you through it, do that instead of bluffing. Know your worth and know that you are worth a real commitment. You are a Queen not a concubine and you should be respected and treated like a Queen.

If he leaves you trying to call your bluff and you don't budge and then he comes back, it's okay to let him come back as long as he is coming back on your terms and respecting your time and your life. Life is too precious to waste years with a man while he is making up his mind. Have him make up his mind on his own time. You aren't being mean or rude; you are showing him that you love and respect yourself and that you know what you deserve as a woman. If you don't show him that you know your worth then you will never get what you are worth.

Make him step up in your life or step out of your life.

14

✼ How to Escape if the ✼ Relationship Won't Work

"Hanging onto someone who isn't adding value to your life isn't loyalty, its stupidity."

The Exit Strategy: It's important to know when it's time to leave. If you've been with a man for more than a year and you seem to hurt more than you are happy, it's time to leave. If you've given him all you can and he is still taking you for granted, it's time to leave. If you have shown him that you are "wife ready" and there still aren't any signs of a life long commitment, it's time to leave. If he is abusing you in any way, it's time to leave. If he's cheated time and time again and doesn't seem to be changing, it's time to leave. If he's promised and lied over and over again and still is doing the same ole things, it's time to leave.

There comes that time when you just know that you have to get out of the relationship. You know it's holding you back and it's driving you to an early grave. Stress is not good for the mind or body and it doesn't help you have a productive and fulfilling life. It's time to let it go. **The exit strategy** is a simple plan that you craft out in your mind. You start a few months before the date you want to be gone and you start building a plan that details where you will go, where you will live, how you will get there, and what are you going to say and do when he comes chasing after you. For you ladies that are stay at home moms or housewives then it's important that you start saving your allowance or whatever you call it. If you have access to the accounts and you pay the bills then start slipping some money into a separate account so that you have some saved up and you're able to pay first and last months rent at your new place and get set up. After all, you are earning the money anyway for all that you're doing around the house and for this man. Your plan has to be airtight and you have to count the cost. It must be thoroughly planned out and you can't miss a step. Choose the day and time you will leave. Decide who you are going to tell that you are leaving. If you have a job then you need to let the security department at your job know that you are leaving a toxic relationship and that you will need someone to walk you to your car each day for a couple weeks. Or you can take off work for a week after you leave so that if he goes to the job and doesn't see you for a week straight he will think that you've quit it too.

After you've escaped this toxic relationship then you can have a phone conversation with him. Be strong, be kind, and be confident. Know what you're going to say before you get on the phone and know that no matter what he says, your mind is made up. Make sure your tears are all gone because you can't show a man any signs of weakness during this call. He needs to know that you are a woman fed up and that you mean business. He needs to be able to sense in your voice that if he tries any foolishness, he's going to jail. Men will huff and puff, yell and curse, beg and plead, or pout and cry, it all depends on what type of man you're dealing with. No matter what he does your mind must be made up that it's going in one ear and out the other. Don't listen to the promises that you've fell for a thousand times.

Understand that if you were sexually active with this man that you've created a **soul tie**. A **soul tie** is a bond that is formed when you become sexually active with a person and it links your souls. The side effects when you're trying to break it are sleepless nights, a weak stomach, a busy mind, tears, pain, and sorrow. It will hurt! You will cry at night. Please understand that you must go through it. Don't try to drown it in alcohol, or with friends and family, or parties and clubbing. Go through it! Cry until you can't cry anymore, hurt until you can't hurt any more. Know this, time heals all things. Each day you will get a little bit stronger. It may take you six months; it may take you a year. You just have to be willing to go through it. You will come out on the others side like pure gold. *When you can't get over it, can't get under, or can't get around it, you must go through it!* Make up your mind that you won't look back!

It's important that you understand the seriousness of this step! Studies show that relationship stress affects the body more than any other form of stress. More than work stress, school stress, more than any other type of stress. Studies also show that individuals who suffer from relationship stress have a much higher chance of dying a premature death of natural causes. Literally, your life depends on this. Toxins can kill you and so can a toxic relationship. Knowing that, don't look back!

The last chance: I know what I just talked about is ideal and what I wish every woman had the strength to do, but the truth is that not every woman has that type of strength. Some women have so many insecurities that they don't know how to stand on their own two feet and be alone until someone better comes along. Some women have been stripped down to bare nothing by that man and don't feel that they are worth anything. Therefore when he comes begging, they usually give in. If you feel like that might be you then I want to teach you how to tell if a man is really sorry after you've left. If you made up in your mind that you're going to leave or if you've already left then I commend you for taking that step. If you don't know if you can stay gone, then this is for you. First I want you to understand that by leaving you are stopping that negative behavior that he exhibits and that's a good thing. By leaving you are telling him that what he's been doing isn't acceptable and that if he wants you to stay then he must change. On the other hand when you stay with a man that isn't treating you right you are telling him that it's perfectly fine. Your presence sanctions the environment that you're in. When you leave then you are telling him that it's not where you want to be and that he must make a change so that you will want to be there with him. For some men, you leaving is a strong enough sign to make him change! Some men will get the picture and change so that you will come back. Others will say they will change and then you go back and it's fine for a week and then it's worse than before you left. You have to know what type of man you have. In the early part of my marriage my wife left me for one day and then came back and I've never messed up again. So I know for sure that your being woman enough to leave can work if you know he is really a good man but just needs to be put in his place. When he comes back begging you can't just dive in his arms and forgive him. You have to let him beg for a little bit. I call this the **72-hour rule.** This is where you let him beg, plead, and do whatever else he's going to do over these three days. Do not forgive him or give in under 72 hours. These 72 hours will allow you to see his range of emotions. You will see if he stays calm or if signs of the old him flares up. If he shows signs of the old him then you let him wait even longer. Tack on time in 72-hour increments and watch his cycle. This 72-hours is not concrete and the reason for that is because men will read this book too and know that you are watching him for 72-hours and he won't show any signs because he knows what you know. So don't give in under 72-hours but have another day amount in the back of your mind just in case you think your man has read this book also. I say that because that's what happened with my **3-month rule** that I published in 2007 in my first book *What Daddy Never Told His Little Girl,* which was later published in Steve Harvey's book, *Act Like A Lady, Think Like A Man,* as the *90 Day Rule* in 2009. I thought I made up that rule as I was writing my book and essentially it was the same thing as Steve's *90-Day Rule,* but what happened is men caught wind of it and started going into relationships not expecting any sex for at least three months. So because they weren't in expectance they never fully got engaged in the relationship until day ninety-one and on day ninety-one most men were getting some and then they left the woman on day ninety-two or day one hundred and then women were upset and blaming the *90-day rule* for their man leaving. So I say all that to say, nothing is concrete because men have access to this knowledge also so go in knowing that and have a counter-plan.

Over this time period that you allot to watch this man's behavior you will see his emotions go up and down and all around like a roller coaster if he hasn't changed. One minute he will be nice and the next he will be cursing you out. Don't let your emotions go on a roller coaster ride with him. Instead pull your emotions out of it and just observe his ride. If anything let it be comedy to you and give you a good laugh. Do not take this grown boy seriously or you will stress yourself out. Take mental notes of how he interacts with you. Study him, observe him, and be patient. Let him feel the pain and let him know that you are serious this time.

If, indeed, he has changed, over this time period you will see a new person. He will be sincere, kind, and respectful. He will reach out to you often but he won't be forceful. He will respect you and give you some space to think about it. If you feel in your heart that he has changed for the better then it's okay to grant him a phone con-versation or to meet him in a public spot like a coffee shop. Don't let him pick you up or drop you off. Drive yourself, and leave by yourself. This is starting over. Take it slow. If you jump right back into what you just got out of then he won't take you seriously and he will call it all a front or a bluff to break up. If he feels that way then he will hurt you worse this next time around out of revenge for playing with his emotions. So take it slow so that he knows you are serious. Let him court you all over again or for the first time if he didn't court you in the beginning. Start over and let him do it right. Build a real friendship. Set boundaries and guidelines and let him know up front and in a real way what you will and won't tolerate. Make sure that he knows you mean business. Men are tough, they can handle the truth and the more real you are with your truth the more they will respect you. If you show a man that you are weak or a push over he will take advantage of you. It's just the hunting nature in a man.

If you try this and he still shows you that he hasn't changed and that he is unwilling to change, then you must let him go for good. Don't let him know where you live, change your phone number and don't let him pop up on you when you are out and about. Carry mace with you and keep someone on speed dial. If he comes up to you in public trying to stop you, keep walking like you don't see him. Men can get a little dumb at times but they aren't crazy. If he does turn out to be crazy then call the police on his butt and don't be afraid to lock him up. Sometimes that's what a man needs to set him straight. This is very serious so I advise you to call the law if you feel your life is in danger. You can't take that into your own hands. Nor do I assume any responsibility for his or your actions this is just to help.

If you have no other guide or no other idea of how to handle this toxic man then I hope this is sufficient. I've taught many women these things and it always works when executed the right way. The only downfall is when women do half of it and not the rest or they start and then let their heart get in the way. This is chess not checkers so play wisely!

15

🎀 *Forgetting Your Ex and* 🎀 *Getting Ready for Your Next*

"You can't see your NEXT if you're too busy looking at your EX. Live life forward"

So many women leave a relationship but they keep one foot in it. When you decide to leave a man then you have to leave that man. You won't be able to see the man in front of you if you are looking back at the man behind you. This happens so often and it's frustrating to good men who are trying to win the heart of a nice young lady but he can't because she's too stuck on the grown boy in her past. If you know that your ex isn't the man you want to marry or the man you need in your life then make up your mind and let him go! There is a man who is watching you everyday but he can't see your true beauty through your frowns. He knows your worth but he's hoping and waiting for the day that you'll realize what you're worth. When letting go of an ex you have to let him go all the way. Throw away all of the old pictures, and all of the things that remind you of him. Throw away all of his t-shirts and everything that he bought for you. If it's expensive then donate it. If you have a tattoo then get it covered up. If you've made up your mind that you are moving on then move on! The only way to forget something old is to replace it with something new. To put it simple, you need something else to do. Hang out with your friends and its okay if you accept new male friends. As long as you aren't having sex with them you are okay. Start focusing on you. Rekindle all of the things that you wanted to do but put off because you were with that toxic grown boy. Focus on your gifts, your dreams, your goals, and start pursuing them. Rebuild your self-esteem and regain your self-worth by stepping out and moving towards your dreams. Make a concrete plan for your life and take action. If you wanted to go back to school then do it. If you wanted to start a business then do it. If you wanted to change your career then do it. Focus on you and start doing the things that you've been wanting and waiting to do. Once you start doing this then you will begin to feel a peace and a complete feeling about yourself. *It's important that you know that it's not a man's place to come into your life to complete you but instead he should come into your life and complement you. If you make a man your everything then when he is gone you won't have anything left.* So focus on you and your family and start fresh.

In this space it's important that you get relationship coaching. I say relationship coaching because in my opinion it's much better than counseling. Counseling is a profession, but coaching is a passion. There is a difference between the two. I'm a Relationship Coach, not a counselor. Counselors go to school and read books on the subject and then teach you what they read. A coach lived through these things and then teach you about what they lived. There is a big difference between reading a book about it and actually living it. So I recommend coaching. The purpose of receiving coaching is so you can go over your past relationship and analyze where you went wrong. Jog your memory, learn from your mistakes and then recondition your mind for the marathon ahead. It's called getting in shape. Learn where you went wrong and then learn what you need to do to get it right. There were mistakes you made in that last relationship that really dictated the outcome of it. Women have all the power in a relationship. The problem is only a few women know that and know how to use it. A man can only do what you let him do and he will treat you the way you allow him to treat you. So, essentially men love women as much as a woman loves herself. Men treat women the way they see women treat themselves. So, if you learn how to treat yourself and how to love yourself then the men who come into your life will do the same. My wife helped me learn how to love by what she stopped, and what she reinforced. She stopped the negative behaviors and she reinforced the positive ones. Naturally any behavior that is recognized and rewarded will repeat itself so it's important to learn what to reinforce and what not to reinforce. Once you've gained this knowledge then you can move on to your physical appearance so that you can begin to attract men. Men will see you before they get to know you. Therefore it doesn't matter how stable you are on the inside if you aren't presenting yourself properly on the outside. Men are visual creatures. Never forget that fact! Remember to refer to the section early on in the book about dressing how you will be addressed. It's important to know what a man is looking for and what will catch his eye, also how to keep him after you've caught him.

Prepare and Position: To prepare, you have to get yourself ready mentally, emotionally, and physically. There are a lot of women who are partially prepared but that's not good enough. It will do you no good to be physically prepared if you are not emotionally prepared. Nor will it do you any good to be mentally, and emotionally prepared if you are not physically prepared. Everything affects everything. If one part is lacking then it will begin to affect the other parts. To get mentally prepared you must learn the ways of a man, not so that you are thinking like a man but so that you understand a man. You can process this information better by actually thinking like a woman. You must learn what to do and what not to do and what to allow and what not to allow. Then you must get emotionally ready. This means you have to give yourself time to fully heal from your past hurts before you move on. Your heart must be at 100% because it will take all of it to make the next relationship work. If you are still crying uncontrollably then you won't be able to keep the next man you come in contact with. If you are still emotionally scarred or torn then you won't be able to appreciate the man that comes into your life. This is very important to be emotionally prepared. Lastly you must be physically prepared. Not many women want to buy into this part but it's very important to be physically prepared because men are visual creatures. You can have the best heart and personality in the world but if your body isn't in tact then a man will pass on you. Men are not built like women so therefore men do not gage your worth with their heart first. It begins with a man's eyes. If he likes what he sees then he is willing to give it a shot. That is why so many women say it's the "bombshell's" or "fake women" that get all the men. It's because those women appeal to a man's eyes and then because men are not emotional creatures they can get over what the woman lacks on the inside. But the interesting thing about it is that a lot of those women who have their body in tact also have good hearts and nurturing traits because those things are innate in a woman. So that is why it seems that those women are winning. Then the women who are overweight or all natural seem to be lagging behind in the men department. This is something you can control. You've never eaten anything by accident, so you can't blame anyone but yourself if your body isn't where it needs to be. I appreciate my wife so much for her efforts because she understands that men are visual creatures and she was determined to do something about it. My wife was what you would call "chubby." She gained weight when she had my son and she had extra skin and baby fat in her tummy area, the back of her arms, back, etc. She made a decision one day that she was going to get fit. A few months later after dieting and exercising properly she has lost like 40-60lbs. Now she is a brick house! I mean she is stacked nicely!! I love and appreciate her for that because she already has my heart and a ring on her finger so she could have easily gotten complacent and I wouldn't have went anywhere. But she understood that men are visual creatures and she did something about it. If every woman would understand this and commit herself to getting in shape and staying that way then the competition would be a lot stiffer out here. It's not fair that men are so visual, but it's a reality. So you either adapt to it or you wait and get what's left over. It's a harsh reality. Like the saying, *it's tight but it's right*. I wouldn't lie to you.

After you are prepared then you must be positioned. To position yourself I mean that you have to create habits and routines that expose you to men. You have to get out and about. You won't be found by your man if you only go to work and then come home and that's all you do. You have to position yourself. So look at your schedule and identify a time that you can walk through the mall for an hour. Also identify a day that you can go to a chill spot and read a book. It can be a coffee shop, a lounge, or a park that is used for exercising or picnics. The reason for this is so you can be seen by single men and be approached. If you are prepared then you will get approached! I recently encountered a perfect example while in the Beverly Center in Los Angeles. I was walking through the mall to pass time and decided I wanted to get something to eat. I went to one of the little lunch spots inside of the mall where you seat yourself and as soon as you walk into that section there are these small tables that seat two. Well there was a female sitting alone at the second table, so I sat at the first one. She was there the whole time that I was there eating. I was close enough to her that if I were single I could have spoken to her using my inside voice. Since I'm a relationship coach who teaches on preparing and positioning it stood out to me that she was sitting alone eating lunch—the perfect way to be approached by a man. I also noticed that she didn't have a ring on her finger. She was prepared. She had on some nice heels, some form fitting jeans, a form fitting shirt, and a cute blazer over it. She had a nice clutch purse, and a head full of weave with curls in it. She was well put together. I'm a married and faithful man and I noticed all of that so imagine what a single man would have done; my point exactly. Not only was she prepared but also she was positioned. She was sitting at a table eating lunch all alone instead of with a bunch of people or with another person. Had I been single I would have spoken to her to strike up a conversation because she was alone and so was I. But if she would have been with a girlfriend then I wouldn't have said anything because it would have been rude to interrupt her and then women like to act stuck up sometimes in front of their girlfriends. I could feel that she was sitting there and hoping that I would say something and also that she was hanging around because she was completely done with her food and just sitting there doing nothing. I'm married so I ignored it, finished eating and then I got up to walk around the mall. While walking around the mall I passed her about three times. I was like wow, she is really positioning herself, and she is doing a great job. She wasn't buying anything because her hands were empty each time I passed her. She was just walking around exercising and window shopping but also positioning. I rarely see females just walk through the mall for an hour window-shopping all alone, but I noticed it that day and I was able to see the technique I teach in action. I really felt like she had to have taken my "Love School" that I teach by phone on Wednesday nights to women. Of course I wanted to flatter myself into believing she was prepared and positioned because of me, but even if she hadn't taken my "Love School" I realized she was doing a great job.

So there you have it. That's a prime example of how to be prepared and positioned. I hope that at some point a nice single man approached her, but if not I know that with that technique one day a man will. It's okay to give your number out; it's not your address. If you give it to a guy and after the first couple of conversations he turns you off then just stop answering his calls and he will get the hint. Give it to as many guys as you can keep up with without mixing up their names. If it's five or ten, it's cool because you need prospects. Trust me; men always have at least three prospects. Even when men are dating they have other women that they are talking to so they can see which one they'd want to settle down with. As a lady you can do the same thing. Don't just zone in on one guy and ignore the red flags and call it "getting to know him." Then the next thing you know a year as passed and you are in no better place than where you started but you've given him a year of your time and some sex. So take all comers and then start to narrow them down. As long as you aren't having sex with any of them then it's okay. You are okay and you are doing it the smart way. Never put all your eggs in one basket until you know that's the basket you want to keep. That's why men always seem to come out on top in relationships because we don't put all our eggs in one basket too soon. The bad thing about men is that men sometimes are sleeping with all their prospects and that's where things get sticky. But as a woman who is 10% smarter than a man and uses both hemispheres of her brain I don't expect you to make the same stupid mistakes men make. So play it smart and play it safe. The way that you need to go will be highlighted throughout the process.

Have fun forgetting your ex and meeting your next!

V
A Winning Marriage

"If marriage isn't the goal then what's the sense in dating?"

16

🎕 *Communication is to* 🎕 *Marriage What Oxygen is to Life*

Communication in marriage is key. If you want your marriage to work then you must be willing to communicate everything that you are feeling. Communication isn't placing the blame or criticizing. Communication isn't yelling or arguing. Communication is telling your spouse how you feel in a cool, calm, respectful manner. Communication isn't just telling your side of it, but it's also listening to their side of it. Communication is seeking to understand them first and then asking them to understand you. The funny thing about communication is that when you take the time to understand their side of it you don't feel the need as much to make them understand you. Communication is leading by example and letting your partner know how you like to communicate or how you two should be communicating. Not many men will naturally communicate the way I just described so sometimes you will have to show him by setting an example and by stopping him when he is communicating in an unacceptable manner. If it's a peaceful time then you should share information with him instead of waiting until you're in a heated debate or disagreement to try and teach him how to communicate. Without knowing any better we've all yelled or pointed the blame at some time. But now that you know better you have to do better. A man will adapt to the correct way of communicating if you don't reinforce any other way.

My wife helped me learn how to communicate by walking away from me if I began to raise my voice at her when we were dating. She would simply put her finger in the air and say, *don't talk to me like that,* and if I continued she would walk away. This taught me that in order to talk to her I would have to talk to her with respect or else I would end up talking to myself. I chose really quickly to talk to her with respect. As long as I was speaking respectfully she would listen for hours if I had that much to express. I also had to teach her how to communicate because she would hold her feelings in until she was about to explode. So I would pull it out of her and I wouldn't leave until she expressed herself in full sentences. Then we both had to learn together not to always refute what the other person was saying but to listen intently and seek to understand. Now we communicate effectively effortlessly. We don't argue any more. There are no screaming matches. There are disagreements and misunderstandings but we work through them like mature adults and we always come out better on the other side. I'm twenty-seven and she's twenty-five and we have mastered this after nearly five years of marriage and about six years of being together. So I'm comfortable and if neither of us take a "stupid pill" we will be together until death do us part as we vowed. Communication is the key!

Rules to Communication

- Communicate in a time of peace not war
- Wait at least an hour after an incident occurs before you address it
- Talk in a quiet and private area i.e. your home
- Listen twice as much as you speak
- Seek to understand first and then to be understood
- Use "I feel" statements instead of "You don't" statements
- Remember that there are no "buts" in apologies
- Do not yell or over talk your spouse
- Make eye contact at all times
- When it's done leave it there
- Forgive and forget (don't bring it up anymore)
- Respect your spouses opinion and or wishes
- Remember the difference between opinions and facts
- Never assume
- Never speculate
- Don't curse
- Always reinforce positive communication
- Never reinforce negative communication
- Lead by example
- Reciprocate Respect
- End on a good note

If you can go over those things and get them deep inside of you and practice effective communication you will save your marriage before it's ever in danger. Do not expect your spouse to know these things, this is not common knowledge so be willing to teach him or share this section with him if you need to. If he can't be approached with outside information then you may need to rethink if you want to spend a lifetime with this man. It's my hope that the two of you can perfect these techniques and strengthen your relationship.

17

❊ How to Keep Your ❊ Husband from Cheating

First what I want you to do is read the section about why some men cheat! If you've read that then those techniques will apply here too. Respect self, remain unpredictable, and occupy time are all in that section and tips that I firmly stand by. My wife has perfected them and it really keeps me on my toes and always interested in her. There are no sure fire ways to stop a man from cheating, but I titled it that with the hopes that you can approach this with optimism. If a man has married you that's the first sign that he wants to do right. Now he just needs all the other pieces of the puzzle to connect to keep him on track. I think every man has a short attention span to anything in life other than sports, or crafts that he enjoys. Women are our favorite but even sometimes we get bored with women. So what a man needs is for his wife to always keep it hot and encourage him to keep it hot too. If your man suggests that you are packing on the pounds you probably want to run to a gym right away. The same goes for the man! If you suggest that he is gaining weight and that he needs to tighten up he probably will. I always tell women that there is another woman waiting for you to slip up. If she gets to know your man in some way she wants to see what areas you are slacking in that those are the areas that she's going to make her strong points. Men stupidly fall for this very often! That other woman could be a mess in every other area of her life but as long as she highlights that she can do what you aren't doing and that she is something that you aren't then she feels she has a chance. The wrong argument with the hubby or the wrong day, she could luck up and catch his attention. Marriage is a job that you can't retire from! You have to come ready to work every day! The beauty about it is that you can do it if you really want to. Women have that strength and ability to balance many roles at once in a very seamless way. Men sit back and watch in amazement.

Here are some tips for you. Your husband loves you, which is clear because he married you. So he loves who you are as a person so just keep your personality in tact and enhance on it if you can. Don't get complacent just because he married you! You know there is such a thing as divorce. So the main things you have to worry about are the outside and your sex life. Keep him guessing! Change your hairstyle as often as you can afford to. I don't mean from short to long if it's your real hair, but from a bun to curls to different ways you part it or style it. Each time you change your hair you look like a different woman and he has to fall in love with you all over again. Take it from me; it's a sexy move! If you wear glasses then see if you can also wear contacts. If you wear contacts then see if you can get another color that goes well with your skin tone. Just a quick side note, if you are a dark skinned woman, do not get blue contacts!!!

Keep it natural. Get an eye color that other people with your skin tone actually have that color naturally. I'm a black male but I have hazel eyes. It's rare but it's natural. As long as there is more than one person with that color then it's considered natural. My wife has dark brown eyes and she wears glasses and contacts so she switches it up and gets honey brown contacts and her eyes pop! She looks so sexy and like a totally different woman and it makes me just want to eat her up. If you don't wear glasses or contacts then that's fine, you can toy with lashes are that proportionate to your face and eyeliner that makes your eyes come alive. Remember your eyes are the windows to your soul, so make them beautiful.

Next you want to work on your body. It doesn't have to be anything crazy, just keep it sexy. I'd say consult a nutritionist and a trainer and get a diet plan and a work out plan. My wife is a trainer now and she is helping a lot of people with their diet and exercise so that they can experience that same feeling she had when she lost her weight. Heck, follow her on twitter @TheExtraRep and email her for a plan if you don't know anyone else- TheExtraRep@gmail.com . Lol, sorry about that plug but I'm passionate about this. We need marriages to work these days! After you get a plan, stick to it. It'll inspire your husband to see you working out and taking care of yourself and he will want to jump on board sooner rather than later so that he doesn't get left for another man. Your body will change if you are diligent about it and it gives a man a feeling that I can't put into words. I'm still young so my body reacts every time I look at my wife and that keeps me so focused on her. The excitement that your man gets from seeing your body in shape will have him wrapped around your finger, IF he has the rest of the package which means if his head is on straight and he's focused in his own life. They say nothing can keep man faithful, if Halle Berry got cheated on but I don't believe that. We don't know what else Halle has going on behind closed doors. And besides your man isn't her man so just because he cheated doesn't mean your man will cheat. Remember a man doesn't cheat because something is wrong with you; he cheats because something is wrong with him. So if your man's head is on straight then, staying on top of your game will definitely help keep it on straight.

After your body is where you want it to be then stay on top of your fashion. No matter what your budget is there is a store that you can afford to shop at and look nice. The key to piquing a man's interest with fashion is to wear colors and sequences that pop. Don't get stuck on black and browns all the time. It's boring and dull if that's all you wear. Make your clothes pop! Stay hip and up to date. Wear things that will accentuate your assets. Switch it up also. If you are known for dressing a certain way then dress the opposite way sometimes just to throw him off. It sounds like a lot but once you plan it out it'll become second nature. Wear leggings one day, a skirt the next, form fitting jeans the next, and then boyfriend jeans the next. It's as simple as that.

Next is the sex life. Men like a woman to take the lead sometimes so if you always wait on him to make a move then switch it up and you make the first move sometimes. If you always make the first move then pull back and play hard to get a couple times. Keep it fresh and keep it hot. It's your husband so ravish in his love and make the most of it. You can't afford to be shy in the bedroom. What you won't do another woman will. Always remember that. Men are very sexual creatures, you know that so make sure that you keep it hot and steamy in the bedroom. I'm not trying to make this a freaky book so I won't elaborate. You get the point! If not then there are some sexperts out here that will give you all the tips you need.

Keep him on his toes and keep him guessing. That's the name of the game. I know some of you are sighing and saying *'why do I have to do all of this to keep a man?'* No one said marriage would be easy. We have to take pride in pleasing one another in our marriage for it to work. I go all out in mine in every area! I keep a six-pack of abs, I keep nice clothes, I stay hot in the bedroom and I'm always buying gifts and speaking her language of love. I will have these same tips and insights for your man in my book for men so don't worry, you will not be the only one working. Remember this is not a guarantee that it will keep your husband faithful but at least you know that you are doing all that you can! By doing this you are decreasing the chances of being cheated on and increasing the chances of having a long-lasting marriage.

It's tight but it's right!!

18

Are You Dependent, Independent or Interdependent?

This is not only for married women but also for women who want to be married. It's very important to know the difference between dependent, independent, and interdependent. In this society women are becoming very independent and being too independent minded can hinder a marriage. A marriage is a team! So in order for it to work you have to understand the difference. Men want to be needed because men naturally have a desire to provide for their family. If a woman will not let a man be a man and bring something to the table then the man will not want to be there. Let me break the three levels of dependency down.

Dependent is the state of a child. Sadly there are some adults that are in this state. This is also the state that a grown boy will want a woman in because he will want you to need him for everything and feel like you are nothing without him. As humans we should only be dependent if we have no other choice, i.e. a life changing accident that leaves you disabled. Other than that we should seek higher levels of dependency. If you do not work and you do not have an education to work or have acquired any skills to work and your man pays all the bills and brings in every cent into the house then you are a dependent. There is a difference between not working and not being capable of working so don't get them confused. You can be a house-wife but be capable of working if you ever got a divorce, that's not a dependent. You are a housewife so technically you are bringing a lot to the table and holding up your end of the bargain. You can get a job in the event that something happens to your man. My suggestion to women is even if you are a housewife you should create some type of income. Whether it's babysitting for other moms who have to work, selling on eBay, or knitting and sewing, do something! Do something so that you can have some stake in the relationship. Do not be a sitting duck. It disables you and makes you weak as a person. If a man is not fully matured and still has some grown boy tendencies then he will feel that whatever he buys he owns and if he has technically "bought" you then he will feel that he owns you too. To be a dependent by choice as an adult is the worst state you can be in.

Then you have independent. This is what we see most often be-cause women have degrees and jobs, dreams, goals, and ambition so therefore women are becoming very independent. Some grown boys will want you to be independent so that he can be your dependent. You should not take care of an able-bodied man under any circum-stances. Who cares if he wants to be a rapper, a singer, a pro athlete, an entrepreneur, or whatever, he needs to learn how to balance his dream (or fantasy) and a job! Do not let your independence go to waste by taking care of a man that won't bring anything to the table. Sadly, I see this all the time. The woman is working and paying all the bills and he's lying around the house talking about he can't find a job or he's waiting on his big opportunity. McDonald's is always hiring and if they aren't ready-labor teams let anyone hop in the truck and go do some work. Make his butt go work or go find someone else to be with.

The problem with some independent women is that they haven't learned how to be independent and ready to become interdependent. Instead they've bought into the idea that they won't accept any help and don't need any help. So they go on dates and want to open the door, they want to pay the bill, they want to carry most of the bags from the grocery store, so on and so on. This presents a major problem in the eyes of a man because he doesn't see where he can fit into your life. Again, men want to be needed. He wants to use his muscles to carry the heavy stuff. He wants to show he's chivalrous and open the door. He wants to put his hard earned money to good use and pay for your dinner. He wants to be a man! So let him. To paint a picture of being independent but ready to be interdependent would look like this; you go out to dinner and when it's time to pay you pull out your card but as soon as he says, *I got it,* you say, *oh well thank you very much.* Then you put away your card. That lets a man know that you can pay your tab but you are also lady enough to let him be a man and pay it for you. The independent woman who isn't ready to go to the next level will insist that she pays it and go back and forth with him and then she will just pay it. Because she doesn't understand the male psyche she thinks that she is sending a good message, but in actuality if she is dealing with a real man then she is sending the wrong message. A man wants to know that there is room for him in your life.

The interdependent woman takes the cake! To be interdependent means that you can stand on your own two feet but you are willing to let a man carry you when your feet get too tired. It means that you can sit down when you need to but you can also stand up when you need to. It means that you bring something to the table instead of just sitting at the table with a fork in your hand. In order to have a healthy marriage you must be able to be interdependent. This means you can work and help save money to build for you and your spouse's future but it also means that you can stay at home and have kids when that time comes. You aren't just taking from him and you aren't selfish and only thinking about your dreams and goals. Instead you have both of you in mind and you complement him as a man. My advice to women is that you stay independent as long as you can. Stay independent as long as you have major dreams in you. That may mean not getting married until forty-five or fifty, look at Oprah! Oprah would not be where she is if she got married at twenty-five. Why? Because life would have taken a totally different twist for her. She wouldn't have been able to put her 'all' into her work and work as much as she does. Oprah is a beautiful woman but you can always see the bags beneath her eyes because she works and she works hard. But I believe there will come a day where she will feel that her work is done and then she can rest and I believe it'll be then that Steadman or another man walks her down the aisle and she goes off into a sunset, buys an island and lives the rest of her days in peace and harmony. There is absolutely nothing wrong with achieving your dreams and getting your hard working years out of you before settling down to be a wife and a mom. Most of you will live to see eighty years old so technically you're not even at the half way mark until forty and even when you hit that you have another ten to fifteen years to keep working hard if you choose to! Men aren't going anywhere so do what you want to do while you are independent because a successful marriage has a different agenda and it will no longer be all about you.   Then on the other hand if you are the marrying type then do it early if you wish, whatever floats your boat. At the end of the day, just know what role you play and where you stand in life and you will be just fine.

19

❧ *Learn to Speak Manglish* ❧

Here I want to just point out some things that men say and do that may not always make sense and tell you what it usually means. It doesn't always mean this but most often this is what it means.

It's not you it's me: this means that he's either unhappy with his life and his level of success at the moment. Or it simply means it's another woman. Lastly it means, he's feeling like a baby and needs some attention.

The silent treatment: this means that he found something of yours that he didn't want to, like a letter from your past or saw something on your Facebook or Twitter that has upset him. He is being silent because he doesn't want to seem like a crybaby so he's asking you to "inquire within" so that he can open up after you've begged him to tell you what's wrong after about five minutes.

Long sits in the bathroom: this means that he is sexually frustrated.

Always snapping at you: this means that he is courting another woman and that you should stick close by him and keep him occupied at all times to break it up before it gets out of hand. You also need to check him on it so that he knows you recognize a difference in his attitude.

What do you want from me: this means that you are being very femalish and asking him to go beyond his natural ability in the areas of communication and articulation and he is not able to do so and really wishes you would back off because you are pushing him away.

We need to take a break: This means that he wants to sleep around without having to answer to you or hide it. He hopes you will be celibate and wait around for him, but while on break if he meets someone he likes you won't hear from him again, so if you knew what's best for you then you would move on too.

Threatening to cheat: this means he's already cheating

Accusing you of cheating: this means he doesn't trust you and or he doesn't trust himself and he's cheating or about to.

Let's just be friends: this means that he's not sexually attracted to you

Frequent guys night out: this means that he's getting bored in the relationship and or he's cheating and his boys are covering for him.

Long stares at you: if you've been together for a year or more it means that he adores you. If it's been less than a year then it means he's falling for you. If it's been less than a month then it means he wants you to think he's falling for you so that you will fall for him and give up the sex already.

Ignoring your calls or text: This means he's trying to increase his power in the relationship and decrease yours by making you needy and dependent. If you know best you shouldn't call him more than twice. Or it means he's with another woman, because he can answer the phone around his boys.

You better be glad I'm with you because no one else would want you: this means he feels worthless and wants you to feel worthless so that you will stay with him forever and be his human teddy bear because he is still a grown boy.

If you do that one more time, I'm leaving!: this means that he wants you to walk on egg shells so that he can do whatever he wants and you won't say anything about it because he thinks you are desperate for love. But if you do it one more time, he will leave but he's coming back because he needs you as much as you need him.

Asking you to cut off friends or family: this does not mean that he loves you so much that he wants you all to himself. It means that he hates himself so much and he wants you to hate yourself too so you both can be sick in the head together and enter into a very toxic relationship that is co-dependent so that even when he starts hurting you there will be no one for you to run to because you've cut every-one off.

Checking your phone and email: this means he knows what type of shady stuff goes on in his phone and email so he wants to check and see if you are doing the same thing. If you are he will curse you out and yell at you and make you feel like crap but pretend he's an angel and that you've crushed him to pieces so that you'll spend the rest of your life making it up to him.

The list can go on and on but I wanted to give you a glimpse into some things men say and do that sometimes send mix messages. I described some of them in a lighthearted way but it's still very serious and I meant every word of it. There are other meanings for some of them but the ones I listed are the most common meanings behind them. It's important that you begin to understand men and the things they do because it can save you a lot of heartache and confusion. Women blame themselves for things sometimes where all the blame should be on the man, but if you don't know any better you'll fall for it every time. If there are other things that you just don't understand just contact me and I'll help you sort through it.

20

🦋 *Don't Get Trapped* 🦋 *in a Burning House*

"Don't expect everybody who comes into your life to be there for a lifetime. Some people are only meant for a season."

In this final section for the married ladies who are struggling in their marriage and don't know what to do I want to encourage you. Til death do us part does not mean until your husband kills you. That doesn't mean stay with a man that is causing you so much stress that he will drive you to an early grave. There are many men who got married before their time and for all the wrong reasons. Some men marry a woman for her money, others because she got pregnant, others because of family pressure, some even to receive extra benefits or perks in the army or from the government. Yes there are benefits to marriage. There are many reasons why a man might marry a woman, and some of those reasons are wrong.

You should never feel like you are trapped by this marriage because you signed the dotted line and because you will be embarrassed in front of your friends and family. Your health and your life are much more important than this marriage if it's toxic. If you have given years of your life and you've tried over and over again to get him to grow up and he is still immature, cheating, and or abusive then it may be time to let him go. There are rules to marriage and marriage guidelines and boundaries that can't be stepped out of. If one of you steps out of bounds then essentially the vows become null and void. It's okay to try and work it out by getting couples counseling or coaching and hopefully it works. If it doesn't work and you've given everything you can and now it feels like you are constantly sick in your mind and your body because of this marriage and you can hardly sleep at night and eat during the day then it's time to let it go.

Leaving a marriage is no different in principle than leaving any other relationship, the only reason why I wanted to have this section separate is because many women feel like they can not leave a marriage under any circumstances, but even the creator of marriage allows it if the vows are broken. If you are at that point then I want you to go back and read the section in the book about leaving a relationship that isn't working. Read it and study it, take notes, and then apply them. Because you are married there should be some things for you on the other end of it if you leave. I'm sure you've heard in the news of women getting settlements, alimony, and so on. Those are benefits of marriage that dating doesn't have. If he has been cheating or abusive and you make more money than he does then you should keep notes, pictures or whatever you need so that you won't have to pay him alimony because he broke the laws of marriage. If you have to pay him alimony it's okay because your freedom and sanity is priceless!

My point for this section is that you should not feel like that just because you said vows that you can't leave. A lot of women stay in a marriage and cry their eyes out every night because they fear starting over and breaking free. Staying in that type of situation will feel more like captivity than being alone in your own space. A relationship is supposed to feel like freedom. It's supposed to feel good and make you a better person. If it's not doing that then it's not healthy. Many women are afraid because they have kids in the marriage and they don't want the kids to have to experience a divorce or have to start over or lose the income that the man brings to the relationship. That isn't a good enough reason to stay. Your kids will be much better off seeing their mom stand up for herself and show them what a real woman is than to stay there and let them see you hurting and crying all the time. Your daughter will enter into that same vicious cycle and your son will one day become the perpetrator of that cycle because he will believe that this is how it's supposed to be. You can't tell your kids to do one thing or live one way and then you do the opposite. It won't work because they will end up saying what you said and doing what you did. Setting an exampling is the best way to teach. If your life isn't an example for what you want them to live then it will have no positive affects on them. Sometimes we have to take a couple of steps backwards so that we can see what lies ahead, readjust and then start moving forward.

Don't settle! You have life left and you deserve to be able to live it to the fullest. So take the information from this book and get out of that toxic relationship, then start over from scratch and get yourself in order and when the time is right then **prepare and position** and get ready to live an exceptional life!

GOD BLESS YOU!!

Special Thanks

I give all glory to God for giving me the wisdom, knowledge and understanding to write a book like this in three days. If you don't believe in God for yourself then believe in Him for me because I know He's real! I know there is no way I can do this on my own. I prayed and asked Him to grant me wisdom and to speak through me and to give me a pure, clean, and wholesome message that will help relationships work and this is what was produced. I'm positive that if you apply what you've learned in this book then things will work out for you.

Next I want to thank my Wife for supporting me, and being understanding while I knocked out this book! I also would like to thank my Wife for being the woman she is and helping me become the man I am today. It's been a journey but we've made it this far and it's looking good from here on out.

I want to thank my Daddy for being an extraordinary man and imparting so much wisdom and sound instruction into my life and helping me in those pivotal moments where I could of self destructed. He helped pull me through as my Father, mentor, and Life Coach.

I thank my Mom for supporting me and encouraging me to use my gift of writing and being able to fully express what's on my mind in words. Had it not been for her speaking the knowledge of this gift into my life I wouldn't have written any books.

I want to thank my business partner and amazing friend Wesley for his support and believing in me and helping me bring my projects to life. He may be the only friend of his kind and its mind-boggling to imagine someone being that loyal and supportive.

Glossary

3-month rule: founded in 2007 by Tony Gaskins Jr. and states that a man who is serious about a woman will talk to her everyday for at least an hour and wait up to three months to have sex with her, and that if he does do those two things it's a strong indication that he is serious about being with that woman.

72-hour rule: the three-day waiting period where you make a man wait before you go back to him.

Bump buddy: someone you just have casual sex with

Grown boy: an adult male that has characteristics of a young boy.

Hold me down: a woman that is just for temporary purposes but has the opportunity to become permanent.

Prepare and position: this is where a woman prepares herself for love and then gets out and about in places where she can be found by love.

Relationship Resume: your resume of past relationships and sexual partners.

Reverse Insanity Plea: the attempt to escape trouble by trying to make your accuser think they are crazy.

Soul tie: a bond that is formed when one becomes sexually active with another.

The Exit strategy: a plan of escape out of a toxic relationship.